BOOKS THAT MAKE YOU SMILE

Some facts are funny, some are weird... and some are both!

SQUARE ROOT OF SQUID PUBLISHING

BOOK CONCEPT BY: ALBERT B. SQUID
ILLUSTRATIONS/WRITING BY: ALBERT B. SQUID

Disclaimer:
These facts are meant to be fun and educational. We've done our best to make sure they're true, but remember—science changes, history gets updated, and sometimes funny facts are just plain silly! Always double-check if you're using them for homework.

JANUARY 1

FACT

THERE'S A CLOWN REGISTRY WHERE CLOWNS REGISTER THEIR FACES.

Real clowns paint their unique makeup on eggs and submit them to the Clown Egg Registry in London. It's like copyright... for your face. So if you ever thought clowns weren't serious about being clowns, just remember, somewhere there's a museum full of eggs with creepy smiles.

FACT

THE FIRST COMPUTER MOUSE WAS MADE OF WOOD.

In 1964, inventor Douglas Engelbart created the very first computer mouse—and it was a wooden block with a button and wheels: no lasers, no scroll wheel, no wireless magic. A simple scroll would give him a lot of splinters in his fingers. OUCH!

JANUARY 3

FACT

SOME TURTLES CAN BREATHE THROUGH THEIR BUTTS.

Yep, you read that right! Certain turtles have a super weird ability: when they hibernate underwater during the winter, they absorb oxygen through their cloaca, basically their butt, a body part that's used for both going to the bathroom and laying eggs. So technically... It's turtle butt-breathing.

FACT

PABLO PICASSO COULD DRAW BEFORE HE COULD WALK.

Okay, maybe not exactly, but he did start drawing at age 2, and his first word was "pencil" (in Spanish: "piz"). By the time he was 9, he was painting better than most adults. Basically, Picasso skipped the drawing stick people phase and went straight to genius mode.

JANUARY 5

FACT

IN SPACE, ASTRONAUTS GROW TALLER!

Without Earth's gravity pushing down on their spines, astronauts stretch out, sometimes by as much as 2 inches! But don't get too excited... once they return to Earth, they shrink back down. Tell everyone you are two inches taller than your real height and just add "in space" at the end.

FACT

SOUTH DAKOTA IS HOME TO THE WORLD'S ONLY CORN PALACE.

Yes, it's a real building, covered in colorful murals made entirely out of corn. Every year, it's redecorated with new designs using corn, grains, and native grasses. It's basically a giant corn-themed art project you can walk inside. So if you've ever dreamed of visiting a corn-covered castle... South Dakota's got you.

JANUARY 7

FACT

THE FEAR OF LONG WORDS IS CALLED, HIPPOPOTOMON-STROSESQUI-PEDALIOPHOBIA.

Yes, the fear has a long word for a name. That's like if you are afraid of high places, naming a fear-of-heights "Skyscraperfalloffophobia." Who did this?

FACT

THE EIFFEL TOWER GROWS TALLER IN THE SUMMER.

Metal expands when it gets hot, and the Eiffel Tower is made of iron. So when summer heats things up in Paris, the tower can grow up to 6 inches taller! In the winter, it shrinks back down again. The Eiffel Tower has a lot in common with Astronauts.

JANUARY 9

FACT

YOUR BRAIN CAN HOLD MORE INFORMATION THAN THE INTERNET.

Scientists estimate the brain's memory capacity is about 2.5 petabytes, that is, 2.5 million gigabytes, enough to store millions of photos, songs, and cat videos. That being said, most people can not remember where they put their phone.

FACT

THE AVERAGE HUMAN HAS ABOUT 100,000 HAIRS ON THEIR HEAD.

This is true for most humans unless you're a baby, a bald grandpa, or a shaggy dog reading this aloud. (In which case, congratulations on your literacy.)

JANUARY 11

FACT

A GROUP OF FLAMINGOS IS CALLED A FLAMBOYANCE.

That's right, a flamboyance of flamingos. Could they possibly have a fancier name? These bright pink birds love to gather in large, loud, stylish groups, and the name totally fits. It's like a dance party of birds that all think they are so fabulous.

FACT

THE FIRST VIDEO GAME EVER MADE WAS ABOUT... TENNIS IN SPACE.

In 1958, a scientist named William Higinbotham created Tennis for Two using an oscilloscope, a screen normally used to measure electrical signals. It looked like Pong, but way before Pong existed. Pong is really boring, so Tennis for Two must be extremely boring, but not as much as Tennis for ONE!

JANUARY 13

FACT

The moon smells like gunpowder.

Astronauts who walked on the moon brought back dust that stuck to their suits. When they returned to the lunar module and took off their helmets, they noticed a weird smell: like burnt fireworks or gunpowder. Maybe space cowboys visited the moon many years ago.

FACT

IN JAPAN, THEY HAVE SQUID, MAYONNAISE, AND CORN PIZZAS.

Different countries put their own twist on pizza by using local favorite ingredients to make new flavors. When the moon hits your eye like a big squidy pie, that's amore.

JANUARY 15

FACT

A DAY ON VENUS IS LONGER THAN A YEAR.

Venus rotates so slowly that one full day (one spin) takes 243 Earth days, but it only takes 225 days to go around the sun (one year). That means a year on Venus is shorter than a day! You could get a lot done on a Venus day!

FACT

IN KOREA, THEY EAT LIVE OCTOPUS THAT IS STILL MOVING.

In Korea, people sometimes eat san-nakji, which is raw octopus that's cut into pieces and served immediately. The tentacles are still moving when they arrive at the table because of nerve activity, so diners have to carefully chew them; otherwise, the suction cups can stick to their mouth or throat!

JANUARY 17

FACT

RAIN DOESN'T ALWAYS FALL AS DROPS.

In the right conditions, raindrops can merge into giant blobs, split into tiny mist, or even flatten into hamburger shapes as they fall. A water burger with cheese sounds refreshing!

FACT

COWS HAVE BEST FRIENDS.

Cows aren't just moo-machines, they're social animals! Studies show they form strong friendships and get anxious when separated from their besties. Put two cow BFFs together and their heart rates drop. Moo-ving, right?

JANUARY 19

FACT

THE LONGEST HICCUPING SPREE LASTED 68 YEARS.

A man named Charles Osborne started hiccuping in 1922 and didn't stop until 1990. That's 68 years of nonstop hiccups, about 430 million in total! No one knows what caused it to start... or stop. The most hated man at the theater and probably not allowed in libraries.

FACT

THERE'S A PLANET MADE OF DIAMONDS.

Far, far away in space floats 55 Cancri e, a planet that might be made almost entirely of crystallized carbon, a.k.a. diamonds! It's super hot and shiny. You could be rich if you could first build a rocket to take you 41 light-years from Earth.

JANUARY 21

FACT

There's no sound in space.

This is because sound needs air or another material to travel through. So if you scream in space... no one hears it. Which is a bummer if you drop your space taco.

FACT

KOALAS HAVE FINGERPRINTS JUST LIKE HUMANS.

Even under a microscope, a koala fingerprint looks almost identical to a human's. If a koala committed a crime (like stealing eucalyptus), they would be busted!

FACT

THE LEANING TOWER OF PISA STARTED LEANING BEFORE IT WAS FINISHED.

Builders noticed it tipping after just three floors, and they kept going anyway! They even tried to fix it by building the upper floors taller on one side. If you want to climb it, do not eat too much pizza before the ascent. You may be the tipping point!

FACT

YOU CAN HEAR "RHUBARB" IN THE MOVIES.

In crowd scenes, background actors often mutter the word "rhubarb" over and over to make it sound like chatter. One might think they are talking about how little their pay is as movie extras instead?

JANUARY 25

FACT

YOUR BONES ARE STRONGER THAN CONCRETE.

Ounce for ounce, human bone is about five times stronger than concrete. Basically, you're a walking skyscraper full of feelings and cereal.

FACT

YOUR BODY HAS MORE BACTERIA THAN HUMAN CELLS.

You're not just a person, you're a walking bacteria hotel. Scientists estimate that the average human has about 30 trillion human cells... and 39 trillion bacteria living in and on them. Bacteria hotel? No more vacancies, sorry, we are full.

JANUARY 27

FACT

SPIDERS CAN'T FLY, BUT THEY CAN BALLOON.

Baby spiders shoot out silk and float on the wind to travel long distances. It's called ballooning, and it helps them find new homes. If there is a hurricane, they might find a new home in a different country.

FACT

NASA once emailed a wrench to space.

In 2014, astronaut Barry "Butch" Wilmore on the International Space Station needed a ratcheting socket wrench. Instead of waiting for the next cargo shipment, NASA engineers 3D-printed the wrench design on Earth, emailed the file to the ISS, and Wilmore printed it using the station's 3D printer. Yeah for technology!!!

JANUARY 29

FACT

GOLDFISH CAN RECOGNIZE HUMAN FACES.

Goldfish aren't as forgetful as people say! They can remember people, learn tricks, and even tell faces apart. So yes, your goldfish knows who is picking and flicking boogers in the living room.

FACT

THERE'S A LAKE THAT EXPLODES.

Lake Nyos in Cameroon sits above volcanic gases. In 1986, it suddenly released a huge cloud of carbon dioxide, which smothered animals and people nearby. Scientists now monitor it to prevent another "exploding lake" disaster. It's probably easy to catch fish, just wait for an explosion and let them land in your boat.

JANUARY 31

FACT

PENGUINS PROPOSE WITH PEBBLES.

Male penguins often find the smoothest, roundest pebble they can and give it to a female as a love gift. If she accepts it, they become a couple and build a nest together. Humans give diamond rings; I'd rather be a penguin, it's cheaper.

FACT

THERE'S A LANGUAGE THAT'S ONLY SPOKEN BY TWO PEOPLE.

In Mexico, a language called Ayapaneco was once spoken by only two people. In the 2010s, the last two fluent speakers of Ayapaneco lived in the same village but had a feud and weren't on speaking terms. Efforts were later made to preserve the language and encourage new speakers.

FACT

A SINGLE SNEEZE CAN SHOOT OUT PARTICLES AT OVER 100 MILES PER HOUR.

A sneeze is actually a powerful explosion. Scientists have measured the speed of a sneeze and found that droplets can fly out of your nose and mouth at more than 100 miles per hour. Try having a sneeze race with a friend. Sneeze toward a wall and see whose droplets hit first.

FACT

JELLY BEANS WERE ONCE USED AS WARTIME CANDY.

During the American Civil War, people made a candy similar to jelly beans to send to soldiers. It didn't melt easily and had lots of sugar for energy. The modern jelly bean got its shell coating idea from an even older candy called Turkish Delight. That's a type of candy, not a Thanksgiving dessert.

FEBRUARY 4

FACT

EARTHQUAKES CAN TURN WATER INTO "LIQUEFIED SOIL".

During a powerful earthquake, the shaking can cause solid ground to act like a liquid. This is called "liquefaction." Buildings can tilt, cars sink, and roads ripple like waves. Dirt smoothie, anyone?

FACT

THERE ARE MORE FAKE FLAMINGOS IN THE WORLD THAN REAL ONES.

Plastic lawn flamingos became so popular in the 20th century that they actually outnumber real flamingos. While there are a few million real ones, estimates suggest over 10 million pink plastic flamingos have been made. That's a lot of tackiness!

FEBRUARY 6

FACT

YOUR FINGERNAILS GROW FASTER ON YOUR DOMINANT HAND.

If you're right-handed, your right-hand fingernails grow a little faster than your left-hand fingernails, and vice versa. Scientists think this is because the hand you use more often has better blood flow, which can help nails grow faster. How exciting it would be to watch a fingernail race.

FACT

A GOAT WAS ONCE ELECTED MAYOR OF A TOWN.

In 2019, the town of Fair Haven, Vermont, elected a baby goat named Lincoln as honorary mayor. Lincoln beat out other animal candidates, including a dog and a cat. The vote raised money for a new playground, and Lincoln even had a little mayor's sash. People must be really bored in Vermont.

FEBRUARY 8

FACT

THE SMELL OF FRESH-CUT GRASS IS ACTUALLY THE PLANT'S CRY FOR HELP.

That lovely grassy smell? It's not what you think. When grass is cut, it releases chemicals called green leaf volatiles. These signals warn nearby plants of danger, attract helpful insects, or try to repair the damage. Don't cry about your haircut grass, it'll grow back

FACT

APPLES FLOAT BECAUSE THEY'RE 25% AIR.

Apples may seem solid, but inside they have tiny air pockets, enough to make them float in water. That's why bobbing for apples works so well. In fact, a whole apple can be about one-fourth air by volume. So, tell your grocery store you only want to pay for the apple, not the air.

FEBRUARY 10

FACT

THE SHORTEST WAR IN HISTORY LASTED JUST 38 MINUTES.

In 1896, the British Empire and the Sultanate of Zanzibar fought a war. It started at 9:02 a.m. and ended by 9:40 a.m., with the British being victorious. It was over before their tea water started to boil.

FACT

SANTA FE, NEW MEXICO, IS THE OLDEST STATE CAPITAL IN THE U.S.

It was founded in 1610, over 200 years before the United States became a country. It's also the highest in elevation, sitting at about 7,200 feet above sea level.

FEBRUARY 12

FACT

THE TONGUE IS THE ONLY MUSCLE CONNECTED AT JUST ONE END.

All your other muscles are attached at two ends, so they can pull bones and move joints. But your tongue? It's free at one end and anchored only at the back. That's what gives it the flexibility to twist, flap, roll, and help you talk, eat, and taste your foot when you say something you should not say.

FACT

LIGHTNING CAN HEAT THE AIR TO FIVE TIMES HOTTER THAN THE SUN.

When lightning strikes, it can heat the surrounding air to around 30,000°C (54,000°F). That's way hotter than the surface of the sun! This extreme heat causes the air to expand rapidly, creating the sound wave we call thunder. BOOM!

FEBRUARY 14

FACT

IN ANCIENT ROME, AN EMPEROR MADE HIS HORSE A SENATOR.

Now, historians debate whether it was a serious promotion or just Caligula trolling the Senate. Either way, that horse probably had the best stable office in Rome, and zero paperwork! Imagine a senator who just neighs during debates. Talk about horsing around in politics!

FACT

ICE CREAM USED TO BE A LUXURY ONLY FOR THE RICH.

Before refrigeration, making ice cream was a major event. People had to collect natural ice from lakes and rivers in winter and store it in underground pits. That meant only wealthy people could afford this chilly treat. Yum! Fish-flavored ice cream. It must have been nice to be rich back then.

FEBRUARY 16

FACT

STARFISH DON'T HAVE BRAINS.

But they can still solve problems. Starfish (also called sea stars) use a network of nerves and a kind of "nerve ring" to control their movements and respond to danger. They can even flip themselves over if they're upside down. But do not ask them to help with math homework, ask a crow instead.

FACT

THERE'S A BUILDING IN CHINA SHAPED LIKE A TEAPOT.

In the city of Wuxi, in China, there's a 38-meter-tall (125 feet) teapot-shaped skyscraper. It doesn't pour tea (sadly), but it does serve as an art museum. So yes, in Asia, even the architecture is ready for a tea party. If you plan to visit, bring your bathing suit.

FACT

THE FIRST VIDEO GAME TO HAVE A "JUMP" BUTTON WAS DONKEY KONG.

Invented in 1981, you had to hop over barrels and obstacles. Before that, most games just had simple left-right movement! So basically, Donkey Kong taught us that sometimes, you just gotta jump over your problems, literally. Imagine if life had a "jump" button; Monday mornings would be way easier.

FACT

YOUR NOSE AND FINGERS SHRINK IN COLD WEATHER.

When it's cold, your body reduces blood flow to your extremities to conserve heat and keep your core warm. This reduced blood flow can make these parts temporarily smaller or feel numb, helping prevent frostbite and keeping vital organs protected during winter's chill. No need for plastic surgery.

FEBRUARY 20

FACT

CANADA'S NATIONAL SPORT IS LACROSSE.

You probably thought it was hockey. Lacrosse is Canada's summer sport because it originated with Indigenous peoples in Canada as a traditional game to build community and train warriors. Canada honors that history by keeping lacrosse as an official national sport. Plus, it's fast and fun, kind of like hockey's wild cousin!

FACT

THE COLOR ULTRAMARINE WAS ONCE MORE PRECIOUS THAN GOLD!

Ultramarine blue was made from the rare and expensive gemstone lapis lazuli, mined mostly in Afghanistan. In the Middle Ages, artists and patrons paid a fortune for this vibrant blue, so much so that painters often reserved it for the most important parts of a painting, such as the Virgin Mary's robe. Talk about blue-blooded luxury in art!

FEBRUARY 22

FACT

SOME SHARKS GLOW IN THE DARK.

It's called bioluminescence, and some deep-sea sharks have it. Their bodies create a soft green or blue glow to help them sneak up on prey or communicate with each other. The glow is usually invisible to human eyes. A shark rave would be pretty cool.

FACT

THE WORLD'S QUIETEST ROOM CAN DRIVE YOU CRAZY.

At a lab in Minnesota, there's a room so soundproofed that it blocks 99.99% of all noise. People who spend more than 30 minutes inside report hearing blood flowing and their bones moving. Most people can't stand it. After thirty minutes in that room, people come out trying to lick their elbows. (You just tried it, didn't you?)

FACT

BAMBOO CAN GROW OVER 3 FEET IN ONE DAY.

That's faster than almost any other plant on Earth. Under the right conditions, certain types of bamboo can grow 35 inches in just 24 hours. Wouldn't it be fun to take the day off and just watch it grow?

FACT

MIT'S OFFICIAL MASCOT IS THE BEAVER.

The beaver was chosen because it is nature's "engineer," known for building dams and solving problems with clever engineering skills. So basically, MIT students have a furry role model who's been rocking engineering way before them!

FEBRUARY 26

FACT

VAN GOGH ONLY SOLD ONE PAINTING DURING HIS LIFETIME.

Despite now being one of the most famous and influential artists ever, Van Gogh struggled with poverty and lack of recognition while he was alive. He sold just one painting, The Red Vineyard, before he died. Marketing wasn't his thing, but he did have an eye for color, and an ear for......Maybe not!

FACT

CATS CAN'T TASTE SWEETNESS.

Unlike humans (and dogs), cats lack the gene that lets them detect sweet flavors. That's why your cat isn't interested in candy or cake. Their taste buds are all about meat. If it doesn't taste like chicken, they're not impressed. That's fine. That means more dessert for us Humans and our dogs.

FEBRUARY 28

FACT

THE HUMAN NOSE CAN REMEMBER 50,000 DIFFERENT SCENTS.

Your nose is a super sniffer. Scientists estimate that the average human can identify around 50,000 different smells. Your scent memory is powerful, too. Smelling something familiar can instantly remind you of a person, place, or event. And sometimes you may want to forget the smell of a place, an event, and especially a person.

FACT

LEAP YEARS EXIST TO FIX TIME ITSELF.

Earth takes about 365.25 days to go around the sun. That extra 0.25 day adds up every year, so every four years, we add a leap day to keep our calendar in sync. Without leap years, the seasons would slowly drift out of place. My friend was born in a leap year. He looks 20 years old, but his actual age is 5.

MARCH 1

FACT

THE ARCHITECT LE CORBUSIER WORKED IN HIS PAJAMAS.

Yes, pajamas and sometimes in his birthday suit. He believed comfort fueled creativity. So while he was designing sleek, futuristic buildings, he was basically living the original work-from-home dream.

FACT

KING CHARLES III TRAVELS WITH HIS OWN TOILET SEAT.

According to royal insiders, the king is so particular about comfort that he reportedly brings a personal toilet seat on some trips. It's for his royal hiney.

MARCH 3

FACT

TARDIGRADES CAN SURVIVE OUTER SPACE.

Tardigrades (also called water bears) are tiny creatures with huge survival skills. They can survive boiling, freezing, radiation, and even the vacuum of space. Scientists once shot them into orbit, and they lived. Who would win a fight between a water bear and a cockroach?

FACT

HIPPOS PRODUCE PINK SWEAT.

Their skin oozes a natural substance that acts as sunblock, moisturizer, and antibiotic, and it's pink! Scientists call it "blood sweat," but don't worry, it's not actual blood. It just looks super dramatic. And FABULOUS!!!

MARCH 5

FACT

THE MONA LISA HAS NO EYEBROWS.

Yep...no eyebrows. Historians think they either faded over time or were never painted at all. Either way, she's been giving people mysterious looks for 500 years with a completely blank forehead. No eyebrows, just like grandma. I wonder if she has no teeth like Grandma, too.

FACT

THERE'S A SPECIES OF ANT THAT EXPLODES.

The Colobopsis Explodens Ant has a weird defense system: when under attack, it can blow itself up to spray a toxic goo on its enemies. It's a sticky, gooey, heroic mess. Talk about an explosive temper.

MARCH 7

FACT

THERE'S A CHEESE THAT SMELLS LIKE SWEATY FEET.

It's called Époisses, and it's so stinky that it's banned from French public transport. Yes, this cheese needs its own seat... and maybe its own warning label. People say it smells awful, but tastes amazing, and is also very expensive. Is that Epoisses cheese in your pocket, or did you just run a marathon without socks?

FACT

VIKINGS NEVER WORE HORNED HELMETS.

That whole spiky-hat image? Total myth, invented by 19th-century opera costumes! Real Viking helmets were simple and practical, because horns on your head in battle would be a great way to get grabbed and clobbered. So next time you picture a Viking, ditch the horns unless he's headed to a costume party.

MARCH 9

FACT

THE SMELL OF CHOCOLATE INCREASES BRAIN WAVES.

When you sniff chocolate, your brain releases theta waves, which are the ones connected to calm, happy, and relaxed feelings. That's why chocolate smells so comforting. Scientists call this the "chocolate effect. I have the "chocolate effect" when I eat peanut butter, too. What if I put them together? Double Happy!

FACT

YOUR BELLY BUTTON IS A JUNGLE OF BACTERIA.

Scientists swabbed belly buttons and found hundreds of species of bacteria, some of which were totally unknown to science. One person even had microbes in there that are normally found in Japanese soil. It would be fun to grow a bonsai in your belly button.

MARCH 11

FACT

SOME FROGS CAN FREEZE SOLID AND STILL SURVIVE.

The wood frog can survive being frozen stiff during winter. Its heart stops, its blood freezes, and its body turns to popsicle mode. Then, when spring comes, it thaws out and hops away like nothing happened. Wouldn't it be nice to skip the cold winter like that?

FACT

THE GREAT WALL OF CHINA IS HELD TOGETHER WITH STICKY RICE.

When building parts of the Great Wall, ancient Chinese workers used a mixture of slaked lime and sticky rice to make super-strong mortar. The starch in the rice made it extra tough. Strong mortar AND lunch. Two birds with one stone.

MARCH 13

FACT

THERE'S A WORD FOR WHEN YOUR BRAIN FILLS IN MUSIC DURING SILENCE.

It's called "auditory imagery." If you've ever heard the rest of a song in your head after hearing just a note, that's your brain DJing on its own.

FACT

MARCH 14 IS PI DAY!

Why? Because it's 3/14, and the number π (pi) starts with 3.14. Pi is the ratio of a circle's circumference to its diameter, and it never ends. People celebrate by doing math... and eating pie. Because, NERDS, obviously.

MARCH 15

FACT

A SNAIL'S TEETH ARE STRONGER THAN STEEL.

Snails have thousands of tiny teeth called radula, and they're made of a super tough mineral called goethite. Scientists measured their strength and found they're stronger than steel. But can they bite through a tardigrade?

FACT

IN SOUTH KOREA, THERE'S A SPECIAL DAY FOR SINGLE PEOPLE.

On this single person's holiday, they eat black noodles. Every April 14th, people who didn't get a Valentine's date gather to eat jjajangmyeon, noodles in black bean sauce. It's like an official "table for one" party, with carbs and feelings. Well, there's always next year's Valentine's Day to try again.

MARCH 17

FACT

BANANAS ARE SLIGHTLY RADIOACTIVE.

Bananas contain potassium-40, a natural isotope that's radioactive. Don't worry, it's harmless in small amounts. You'd need to eat about 10 million bananas at once to get radiation sickness. Could you eat 10 million of anything? Maybe rice!

FACT

YOU CAN START A FIRE WITH ICE.

If you carve a piece of clear ice into a lens (like a magnifying glass), you can focus sunlight enough to start a fire. It's tricky, but it works. Why you would need to do this is beyond me. Unless you were stranded at the South Pole.

MARCH 19

FACT

THE PLANET NEPTUNE HAS SUPERSONIC WINDS.

Neptune has the fastest winds in the solar system, over 1,300 miles per hour. That's faster than the speed of sound. Scientists still aren't sure how a planet that far from the sun got such wild weather. There isn't any glue strong enough to keep a toupee on tight with that wind speed.

FACT

COWS CAN WALK UP STAIRS, BUT NOT DOWN.

Cows can physically walk upstairs because of how their legs bend. But going down? That's a challenge. Their knees don't flex the right way, and they get freaked out. So yes, cows can be trapped upstairs. But who lets cows in the house anyway?

MARCH 21

FACT

THERE'S A PLACE IN VENEZUELA WHERE IT STORMS ALMOST EVERY NIGHT.

It's called the Catatumbo Lightning, and it happens for 260 nights a year where the Catatumbo River meets Lake Maracaibo. The unique mix of mountains, warm air, and moisture creates a lightning show that can flash up to 280 times an hour. It's basically Earth's most dramatic light switch.

FACT

SOME PLANTS CAN "HEAR" THEMSELVES BEING EATEN.

When a caterpillar munches on a leaf, the plant actually senses the vibrations and responds by producing bitter chemicals. It's like a leafy alarm system. They are listening! Remember that the next time you eat salad.

MARCH 23

FACT

NAPOLEON WAS ONCE ATTACKED BY BUNNIES.

In 1807, Napoleon planned a fun rabbit hunt for his army. But when the cages were opened, hundreds of rabbits charged at him instead of running away, because the organizers had accidentally bought tame farm bunnies. Napoleon tried to flee, but the rabbits swarmed his boots. What a tough guy!

FACT

THERE'S A FISH THAT CAN WALK ON LAND.

The mudskipper is a fish that can wiggle, hop, and climb using its fins. It lives in muddy swamps and actually breathes air through its skin. Well, there was a HUMAN once who could walk on water, so there mudskipper!

MARCH 25

FACT

THERE'S A SECRET ROOM HIDDEN INSIDE MOUNT RUSHMORE.

Behind Lincoln's head is a Hall of Records, a chamber that was supposed to hold important U.S. documents. It's not open to the public, which means Mount Rushmore technically has a giant stone forehead with a secret brain cave. If it's so SECRET, how come we know about it now?

FACT

NASA'S MARS ROVERS SING "HAPPY BIRTHDAY" TO THEMSELVES.

When the Curiosity rover landed on Mars, engineers programmed it to play "Happy Birthday" using its internal sample analysis equipment. It did it once, on its first Martian birthday in 2013. Since then? No parties. So, technically, an engineer once built the loneliest birthday machine in the solar system.

MARCH 27

FACT

PRESIDENT TAFT ONCE GOT STUCK IN A BATHTUB.

William Howard Taft, the 27th U.S. president, was a big guy, over 300 pounds. One day, he got stuck in the White House bathtub, and they had to build a custom super-sized tub that could fit four men. He wouldn't have needed a custom bathtub if he had just stopped eating all that roasted possum.

FACT

A DAY ON URANUS IS ONLY 17 HOURS.

Uranus may spin sideways, but it does so super fast, just 17 hours per full spin. That's less than one Earth day! No time for homework. Darn!

MARCH 29

FACT

RATS CAN LAUGH.

When rats play or are tickled, they make high-pitched giggle-like sounds that humans can't hear without special equipment. It's one of the weirdest and most adorable facts in science. That's cute, but it doesn't make them any less ugly-looking.

FACT

THE HUMAN STOMACH GETS A NEW LINING EVERY FEW DAYS.

Your stomach produces acid strong enough to melt metal, so to protect itself, it replaces its lining every 3 to 4 days. Otherwise, it would digest itself. It's like changing your underwear.

MARCH 31

FACT

SOME TREES CAN CLONE THEMSELVES.

There's a tree called Pando in Utah that looks like a forest, but it's actually one single organism. All the "trees" are genetically identical and connected by the same root system. It's one of the oldest and largest living things on Earth, and it's been cloning itself for over 80,000 years! Wouldn't it be nice to clone yourself?

FACT

SPAGHETTI TREES WERE ONCE ON TV.

In 1957, a British news show ran a fake story about people harvesting spaghetti from trees, and people believed it and even called in to ask how to grow their own spaghetti plants. It was quite the trick. And also... Happy April Fools' Day.

APRIL 2

FACT

IT WOULD TAKE ONE YEAR TO WALK ACROSS RUSSIA.

Russia is so big that it spans 11 time zones. This means when it's morning in one part of the country, it can already be night on the other side! This makes coordinating things like travel and communication across Russia pretty challenging. And tiresome!

FACT

HOT WATER FREEZES FASTER THAN COLD WATER.

It's called the Mpemba effect, and scientists are still debating exactly why it happens. Under the right conditions, hot water can beat cold water to the freezing finish line. It's like water saying, "I may be hot now... but just you wait.

APRIL 4

FACT

THERE'S A SPECIES OF JELLYFISH THAT LOOKS LIKE A FRIED EGG.

It's called the fried egg jellyfish, and yes, it looks exactly like breakfast. Big yellow center, wobbly white edges, floating through the ocean like a lazy brunch. It might be good on toast with a slice of cheese. Probably not!

FACT

THE INVENTOR OF COTTON CANDY WAS A DENTIST.

Yes, a dentist. Dr. William Morrison co-invented cotton candy in 1897. Maybe he was trying to guarantee repeat customers by selling sugar clouds on a stick. Pretty smart marketing, Doc!

APRIL 6

FACT

SUBMARINES FILL WITH WATER TO SINK.

When the submarine fills its tanks with water, it becomes heavier and sinks. When it pushes the water out and fills the tanks with air, it becomes lighter and rises to the surface. So basically, submarines are like giant, super-smart balloons that can decide when to sink like a stone or float like a bubble.

FACT

SHARKS EXISTED BEFORE TREES.

Sharks have been around for 400 million years. Trees didn't show up until about 350 million years ago. That means for 50 million years, sharks didn't have the chance to build a cool tree fort. But they do now!

APRIL 8

FACT

WORMS CAN HAVE UP TO 10 HEARTS.

Depending on the species, some worms have five pairs of hearts (technically, heart-like organs called aortic arches). It must be crazy on Valentine's Day to give your 10 hearts to 10 different worms.

FACT

TATTOOS WERE ONCE BANNED IN JAPAN.

In the Edo period, tattoos were outlawed for regular folks because they were linked to criminals. But samurai secretly used tattoos as badges of honor and personal expression. So, tattoos in Japan were kind of like a secret handshake for warriors, inked and proud, but under the radar!

APRIL 10

FACT

YOU CAN NOT SMELL YOUR OWN BAD BREATH.

Your brain gets used to your natural smells and just ignores them. That's why you might not notice your own stinky breath, even if it could knock over an elephant. It's called olfactory adaptation, and it's the reason for many divorces.

FACT

EUROPEAN NOBLES WORE SHOES THAT WERE 2 FEET LONG.

These super-long shoes were a way to show off wealth and style, because only rich people could afford to walk with such tricky shoes. So basically, these shoes were like skis attached to your feet, great for 15th-century style, terrible for track and field events.

APRIL 12

FACT

THE MOON HAS MOONQUAKES.

Just like Earth has earthquakes, the moon has moonquakes. Some are caused by meteor impacts, but others come from deep inside the moon. It's like the moon is stretching, sighing, and occasionally saying, "It's so boring being up here alone. Come back, Mr. Armstrong."

FACT

THE FIRST ALARM CLOCK COULD ONLY RING AT ONE TIME.

In 1787, the inventor Levi Hutchins built a clock that rang only at 4:00 AM, because that's when he wanted to wake up. No snooze, no settings. Just one guy, one chime, and one very early morning. Thanks, Levi. I guess.

APRIL 14

FACT

BUTTERFLIES DRINK TURTLE TEARS.

In the Amazon, butterflies have been seen landing on turtles' faces to sip their tears. It's not because they're emotional vampires, it's for the salt. Science is weird. And mildly rude.

FACT

A SINGLE CLOUD CAN WEIGH OVER A MILLION POUNDS.

Clouds may look like floating cotton candy, but they're loaded with water. A medium-sized cloud can weigh more than a million pounds! Luckily, the water's spread out and floats due to warm air currents. Still... heavy stuff floating above your head.

APRIL 16

FACT

SLUGS HAVE FOUR noses.

Well, technically, they have four tentacles, but two of them help them see and two help them smell. That's double the sniffing power of most creatures. So if a slug ever smells your lunch, it's not a coincidence. It's a tactical scent strike.

FACT

THE KETCHUP PACKETS WERE INVENTED IN 1980.

Before that, people used tiny glass ketchup bottles at restaurants. So next time you squeeze ketchup on your fries, remember: you're basically using a mini plastic ketchup squirt gun that replaced the slow, clumsy little glass bottles. Sauce upgrade unlocked!

APRIL 18

FACT

THERE'S A PLANET WHERE IT RAINS GLASS.

Sideways. The exoplanet HD 189733b has winds blowing at 4,500 miles per hour and storms made of molten glass. So if you're planning a vacation there... maybe cancel. Your umbrella won't help you at all.

FACT

SOME PEOPLE CAN TASTE WORDS.

It's called synesthesia, and it's when senses mix. So, someone might say "Tuesday" tastes like lemon. Or "library" tastes like old socks. (Tough snack.). What do you think the word "cheeseburger" tastes like?

APRIL 20

FACT

TOMATOES WERE ONCE CONSIDERED POISONOUS.

In the 1700s in Europe, rich people thought tomatoes were toxic because folks who ate them got sick. But the real problem? The lead in their fancy plates. Turns out it was bad dinnerware, not the tomatoes. Dumb rich people.

FACT

IN JAPAN, SLURPING YOUR NOODLES IS CONSIDERED POLITE.

The louder you slurp, the more you're showing the chef you love their cooking. So yes, what gets you weird looks at home gets you bonus points in a Tokyo ramen shop. The sound may be okay, but what about the splash?

FACT

APRIL 22ND IS EARTH DAY—BUT IT WASN'T ALWAYS GLOBAL!

The very first Earth Day in 1970 started as a U.S. event with 20 million Americans protesting pollution. It took a few years before Earth Day became an official worldwide movement. So, Earth Day's global "green takeover" began with one giant American environmental wake-up call!

FACT

THE FIBONACCI SEQUENCE APPEARS ALL OVER NATURE.

It appears in things like pinecones, sunflower seeds, and even pineapples! This sequence (each number is the sum of the two before it: 0, 1, 1, 2, 3, 5, 8, ...) helps plants pack seeds or leaves most efficiently so they get the most sunlight or space. It's like the secret code of nature.

APRIL 24

FACT

IN THAILAND, IT'S CONSIDERED RUDE TO STEP ON MONEY.

That's because Thai currency has the king's face on it, and feet are seen as the lowest, dirtiest part of the body. Accidentally stepping on a coin or bill isn't just clumsy, it's a royal foot offense! So if your money blows away in Bangkok, chase it with your hands, not your sneakers.

FACT

CANADA HAS THE LONGEST COASTLINE OF ANY COUNTRY IN THE WORLD.

It's over 202,000 kilometers (125,000 miles)! That's so much coastline, you could probably take a daily stroll along the shore and still not see it all in a lifetime. But you would meet a lot of nice folks wearing tuques and say "eh" at the end of each sentence.

APRIL 26

FACT

SIR ISAAC NEWTON'S DOG ACCIDENTALLY RUINED YEARS OF HIS WORK!

The story goes that Diamond knocked over a candle and burned many of Newton's important manuscripts. Talk about a "ruff" day for science. At least he didn't eat the apple, or we might all be floating in the air.

FACT

VENUS ROTATES THE OPPOSITE WAY FROM EARTH.

On Venus, the sun rises in the west and sets in the east. And one Venus day is longer than its year. So if you lived there, mornings would be weird, clocks wouldn't help, and you'd never be on time. Ever!

FACT

ANTS CAN SURVIVE A FALL FROM ANY HEIGHT.

Because they're so tiny and light, ants don't splat when they fall. They just sort of float and land like superheroes. If you dropped an ant from a skyscraper, it would brush itself off and keep walking like nothing happened. That being said, if there is strong wind, they might end up on the other side of the world.

FACT

THE PYRAMID OF GIZA WAS ONCE THE TALLEST STRUCTURE IN THE WORLD.

Built around 4,500 years ago with incredible precision and massive limestone blocks, it was such a feat of engineering that no other building surpassed its height until medieval cathedrals appeared. The cathedrals said, "We're the boss now!" That is, until the skyscraper showed up.

APRIL 30

FACT

MALTESE DOGS HAVE BEEN ROYAL COMPANIONS FOR OVER 2,000 YEARS!

They were favorites of ancient Mediterranean nobility and even appeared in Egyptian and Roman art. So when you see a Maltese, you're basically looking at a tiny dog with royal roots and centuries of being pampered like a true VIP!

FACT

A BABY OCTOPUS IS ABOUT THE SIZE OF A FLEA.

When octopus babies hatch, they're teeny-tiny, practically invisible blobs of jelly. But give them time, and they'll grow into super-smart, shape-shifting sea ninjas. Every big-brained squid starts out as a speck!

MAY 2

FACT

THE "POWER CHORD" IN ROCK MUSIC CAN BE PLAYED BY TODDLERS.

Power chords are simple two-note chords that cut through heavy distortion without sounding muddy, making them perfect for the loud, aggressive sound of rock. They are so simple that even kids can play them easily.

FACT

THE FIRST "FUN FACT" STYLE TRIVIA DATES BACK TO ANCIENT ROME.

Writers like Pliny the Elder made fun tidbits and sayings to entertain people in ancient times. So basically, people have been loving weird and wonderful tidbits for thousands of years, proving curiosity and the joy of random facts are ancient hobbies!

MAY 4

FACT

SLOTHS CAN TAKE UP TO A MONTH TO DIGEST A SINGLE LEAF.

Sloths have the slowest metabolism of any mammal. It can take them 30 days to finish digesting one leafy meal. If humans had the metabolism of a sloth, we could save money on groceries and trips to the bathroom.

FACT

IN THE 1930S, A BRITISH COMPANY INVENTED THE "CAT RADIO".

It was a small radio device designed to be strapped onto cats so they could "carry news reports" around town! The idea was to have cats deliver live broadcasts as they roamed, but thankfully, it never caught on beyond a few prototypes. Definitely one of the strangest concepts in radio history!

MAY 6

FACT

Women generally have better color vision than men.

Since women have two X chromosomes, they often get a "double dose" of these color vision genes, while men (with one X and one Y chromosome) have fewer copies, which is why color blindness is much more common in men.

FACT

YOUR STOMACH GROWL HAS A NAME: BORBORYGMUS.

It's the rumbling noise your belly makes when it's moving gas and fluids around. It doesn't just happen when you're hungry; it's going on all the time, like an embarrassing digestive drum solo.

MAY 8

FACT

THE FIRST 3D-PRINTED ORGAN TRANSPLANT HAPPENED IN 2021.

Scientists created this mini heart that actually beats, paving the way for future organ transplants made on demand. So, the future of medicine might literally be printed, no waiting, just press "start" and go!

FACT

AIRPLANE BLACK BOXES ARE ACTUALLY BRIGHT ORANGE!

They're painted bright orange so that if a plane crashes, investigators can easily spot the boxes among the wreckage.

MAY 10

FACT

CONCRETE ACTUALLY GETS STRONGER AS IT AGES.

Concrete hardens through a chemical process called hydration, where water reacts with cement, and this reaction can continue slowly over a very long time. Concrete is like that one friend who keeps getting better with age, just way less fun at parties and way harder to move when you need to redecorate.

FACT

MOZART WROTE HIS VERY FIRST SYMPHONY WHEN HE WAS JUST 8 YEARS OLD!

By the time most kids are still learning their ABCs, Mozart was already composing full orchestras. A mini maestro in a powdered wig.

MAY 12

FACT

LIGHTNING STRIKES EARTH ABOUT 8 MILLION TIMES A DAY.

That's over 90 times per second! Somewhere, right now, a lightning bolt is lighting up the sky like a paparazzi flash for clouds. Storms don't mess around.

FACT

THE WORLD RECORD FOR THE MOST T-SHIRTS WORN AT ONCE IS 260.

A man in Uganda squeezed into 260 shirts, layer by sweaty layer. By the end, he looked like a walking laundry pile with arms. Look out, kids, it's a t-shirt monster!

MAY 14

FACT

THE FASTEST TIME TO EAT A BURRITO IS 31.47 SECONDS.

Set by a competitive eater named Leah Shutkever, she inhaled a full burrito faster than most people can unwrap it. It was less "lunch" and more high-speed tortilla teleportation. She also holds the record for the fastest run to the bathroom.

FACT

THE LONGEST LIVING ANIMAL IS A CLAM NAMED MING MING.

The clam lived to be 507 years old before scientists (oops) accidentally opened it. It was born before Shakespeare, Galileo, and tacos. RIP, Ming. You were truly shell-shocking.

MAY 16

FACT

THE DOT OVER A LOWERCASE "I" IS CALLED A TITTLE.

Yes, it has a name. No, it's not made up. Tittles are the tiny dots above "i" and "j." Language is weird, ain't it?

FACT

GORILLAS BURP TO SAY, "I'M FULL."

After eating a big leafy meal, gorillas will sometimes let out a loud burp to signal satisfaction. It's not rude, it's polite in gorilla culture. But the smell would knock over an elephant.

MAY 18

FACT

THERE'S A SPECIES OF FUNGUS THAT TAKES OVER ANT BRAINS.

The zombie-ant fungus infects ants and controls their behavior, making them climb to high places so the fungus can grow and spread. It's horrifying. It's fascinating. It's basically fungus mind control.

FACT

YOUR TONGUE PRINT IS AS UNIQUE AS YOUR FINGERPRINT.

No two tongues are the same! If tongue-print scanners were a thing, you'd be licking your way into secret clubs and spy lairs. Mission: Grossible.

MAY 20

FACT

MOST WASABI ISN'T REAL WASABI.

The green stuff you get with sushi? That's usually dyed horseradish. Real wasabi is rare, expensive, and hard to grow. You've probably been eating spicy impostors your whole life.

FACT

WE RECEIVED AN ALIEN RADIO SIGNAL FROM SPACE.

The famous "Wow! Signal" detected in 1977 was a strong, unexplained radio signal from outer space that some scientists think could have come from an intelligent alien source. But despite many attempts, the signal has never been detected again, and its origin remains a mystery! Maybe the alien that called lost its phone, like humans do all the time.

MAY 22

FACT

MILITARY HELICOPTERS WERE FIRST USED IN THE KOREAN WAR.

They were extensively used for medical evacuation (medevac) to transport wounded soldiers from the battlefield quickly. Helicopters could reach difficult terrain and get injured troops to medical care much faster than ground vehicles, saving many lives.

FACT

YOU CAN HEAR RHUBARB GROW.

In spring, some varieties of rhubarb grow so fast that they make popping, creaking sounds as their stalks push through the soil. It's like a vegetable ASMR concert.

MAY 24

FACT

THE HUMAN BRAIN USES 20% OF YOUR BODY'S ENERGY.

Even though your brain is only about 2% of your body weight, it hogs 20% of your fuel. It's like a tiny, wrinkly boss demanding snacks at all times.

FACT

SATURN'S MOON TITAN HAS LAKES OF METHANE.

Not water, liquid methane, which is basically a super cold gas that smells like rotten eggs. If you went swimming on Titan, you'd freeze solid and float in a puddle of alien fart juice. Science!

MAY 26

FACT

SOME BUTTERFLIES DRINK BLOOD.

They're called "vampire butterflies" (yep), and they suck fluids from dead animals—or occasionally open wounds. Beauty and the Beast? More like, beauty IS the beast.

FACT

ARTIST JACKSON POLLOCK PAINTED AN ENTIRE CANVAS WHILE STANDING ON IT!

He famously dripped, splattered, and poured paint all around, walking right on his artwork to create his signature style. It was like dance and painting rolled into one wild, messy performance.

MAY 28

FACT

IRELAND IS HOME TO THE WORLD'S OLDEST KNOWN PUB.

Sean's Bar, which has been serving drinks since around 900 AD, is the oldest known pub! That means people have been enjoying a pint there for over 1,100 years. That's a long time. Sean must be really tired!

FACT

THE HUMAN BODY GIVES OFF LIGHT.

You glow. Slightly. Scientists using special cameras discovered that people give off faint light. We're just too eyeball-limited to notice. So yes, you're glowing, but only in stealth mode.

MAY 30

FACT

FEMALE PRAYING MANTISES EAT THE MALES AFTER OR DURING MATING!

It sounds brutal, but this "mating cannibalism" actually helps the female get extra nutrients for her eggs. So, for the mantis, love can literally be a deadly affair!

FACT

THE MICROWAVE WAS INVENTED BY ACCIDENT.

Percy Spencer was testing radar equipment when a chocolate bar in his pocket melted. He realized microwaves could cook food, and BOOM, the microwave oven was born. Science: Sometimes it starts with a snack attack.

JUNE 1

FACT

MAINE IS THE ONLY U.S. STATE WHOSE NAME IS JUST ONE SYLLABLE.

Plus, it's the easternmost state in the continental U.S., so when the sun rises over the USA, it often first hits Maine! So lobsters get the first sunburn.

FACT

CROWS REMEMBER FACES AND HOLD GRUDGES.

If you're mean to a crow, it can remember you for years and might even warn other crows. If you're nice, they might bring you shiny gifts. Either way, don't mess with a bird that can out-plot you.

FACT

THE TERM "ARTIFICIAL INTELLIGENCE" WAS FIRST COINED IN 1956.

At Dartmouth College, the original researchers thought AI would be solved in just a few decades! Fast forward nearly 70 years, and we're still figuring it out, but look how far it's come! It hasn't taken all our jobs. YET!

FACT

IF YOU FELL INTO A BLACK HOLE, YOU WOULDN'T NOTICE ANYTHING SPECIAL.

But to an outside observer, you'd appear to freeze in time forever! So physics says you'd experience a smooth ride in, but everyone else would just see you stuck at the edge of the black hole. But to be on the safe side, try not to get too close to a black hole.

JUNE 5

FACT

IN SOME PARTS OF ALASKA, IN SUMMER, IT'S DAYTIME FOR 24 HOURS.

The sun never sets for weeks! People call it the "Midnight Sun," so you can have a summer BBQ at midnight without needing flashlights. Summer party, all day and all night long!

FACT

LISTENING TO MUSIC RELEASES DOPAMINE IN YOUR BRAIN.

This is the same chemical that makes you feel pleasure from eating or falling in love. Music stimulates the brain's reward system, triggering dopamine production, which is why songs can give you chills or make you want to dance. Put on the jams and let the party in your brain begin.

FACT

HIGH HEELS WERE ORIGINALLY WORN BY MEN.

Men wore high heels in the 10th century to help them stay steady in stirrups while riding horses. The heel helped secure their feet in the stirrups for better control and balance during horseback riding and combat. Some men still wear high heels today. No judgement!

FACT

BEES CAN FLY HIGHER THAN MOUNT EVEREST.

Scientists have tracked bees flying over 29,000 feet, the height of the tallest mountain on Earth. If they wore tiny oxygen tanks, they could summit Everest and still make it home for honey.

JUNE 9

FACT

SOMEONE INVENTED A PARACHUTE SUIT.

In the 1930s, a man named Franz Reichelt invented a wearable parachute suit. It was basically a parachute you could wear like a coat! He actually tested it by jumping off the Eiffel Tower... but sadly, it didn't work, and he died in the attempt. Maybe he should have tried it with a mannequin first.

FACT

IN 1933, THE FIRST DRIVE-IN MOVIE THEATER OPENED.

It was in Camden, New Jersey, and it quickly became a popular way for families and couples to watch movies from the comfort of their cars! BONUS: The first drive-in movie shown was called "Wives Beware".

FACT

A GIRAFFE'S KICK CAN KILL A LION.

One solid, strong kick from those long legs can send a lion flying. Don't let the cute eyelashes fool you; giraffes are peaceful, but their legs are lethal weapons.

FACT

NORWAY HAS A TOWN CALLED "HELL.

It really freezes over in winter! Hell is a small village, and during winter, temperatures often drop below freezing, making "Hell freezing over" a very real thing. So next time someone says that phrase, you can say, "Actually, it happens every year, in Norway!"

FACT

THE FIRST MOVIE EVER MADE WITH SOUND WAS THE JAZZ SINGER IN 1927.

Before that, movies were silent and often accompanied by live music or narrators, but The Jazz Singer used a new technology to record sound and dialogue along with the film. Nowadays, there's too much sound. Especially with all the phones ringing at the movie theater.

FACT

VATICAN CITY IS THE WORLD'S SMALLEST COUNTRY.

It's called a city, but it is actually a full country. It's only about 110 acres (0.17 square miles), but it has its own post office, radio station, and even a soccer team! So this tiny city-state packs a surprising amount of history, culture, and activity into a space smaller than many amusement parks.

JUNE 15

FACT

THE LONGEST NOVEL EVER WRITTEN IS 4,500 PAGES LONG.

It is In Search of Lost Time by Marcel Proust. It explores the memories and time with long, flowing sentences that dive deep into every thought and feeling. By the time you finish reading it, we may have a colony on Mars.

FACT

EARTH IS HIT BY OVER 100 TONS OF SPACE DUST EVERY DAY.

Tiny bits of rock and dust from comets and asteroids rain down constantly. Most of it burns up in the atmosphere. So yes, your house gets micro-sprinkled with space glitter. You're welcome.

JUNE 17

FACT

THERE'S A BUILDING IN POLAND THAT LOOKS LIKE IT MELTED.

It's called the Crooked House (Krzywy Domek), and it looks like someone hit "warp" in Photoshop and then built it for real. The windows, walls, and roof all curve like a cartoon. It's so surreal, it's hard to tell if you're outside a shopping mall or inside a dream.

FACT

PLATYPUSES ARE venomous.

Platypuses are one of the only mammals that come with factory-installed venom. The males have ankle spurs that can inject a toxin so painful it made doctors say, "Wow, we have nothing stronger for this." So basically, the platypus looks like a cuddly biology mistake... but it's also secretly packing nature's taser in its heels.

JUNE 19

FACT

SOME FISH CAN CLIMB WATERFALLS.

The Hawaiian goby fish uses a sucker on its belly to climb up wet rocks and waterfalls as a baby. They basically go through an obstacle course just to reach their new homes. One might say they are nature's ninja fish.

FACT

PEANUTS AREN'T NUTS.

They're legumes, like beans! True nuts grow on trees. Peanuts grow underground. So they're basically bean impostors wearing nut costumes. What a nutty fact.

JUNE 21

FACT

JUNE 21 IS THE LONGEST DAY OF THE YEAR (IN THE NORTHERN HEMISPHERE).

It's the summer solstice, when the sun stays out longer than any other day. More daylight, more snacks, more time to read weird facts. Science says: go outside and bask. That almost rhymes.

FACT

THE WORLD'S MOST EXPENSIVE PIZZA COSTS OVER $12,000.

It's called the Louis XIII Pizza, made in Italy with rare caviar, lobster, organic buffalo mozzarella, and pink Australian salt. Oh, and it's served by a private chef at your house, because clearly, delivery just isn't classy enough. It's the only pizza where you ask, "Do I eat it… or insure it?"

JUNE 23

FACT

T. REX'S ROAR IN A MOVIE WAS ACTUALLY A MIX OF THREE DIFFERENT ANIMALS.

In a famous dinosaur movie, the T. Rex sound was made by mixing elephant, tiger, and alligator sounds. Sound designers combined these animal noises to create that iconic, terrifying roar, proving movie magic is part science, part weird animal sounds.

FACT

THERE'S A HOTEL MADE ENTIRELY OF ICE.

In Sweden, the Ice Hotel is rebuilt every winter out of snow and ice blocks, then melts in spring. Guests sleep in thermal sleeping bags… on ice beds. It's the world's coldest sleepover party.

JUNE 25

FACT

HORSES CAN'T VOMIT.

Their stomach muscles don't allow it, which makes colic (horse belly aches) really serious. So yeah, horses eat carefully and keep it all in. The good news is we never have to see hay and apple puke.

FACT

ROMANS USED A SHARED SPONGE ON A STICK INSTEAD OF TOILET PAPER.

Romans had public toilets called "latrines" where people would sit side-by-side without any partitions, and they used a shared sponge on a stick, called a "tersorium," to clean themselves instead of toilet paper! Did you notice the word "SHARED"?

JUNE 27

FACT

A NARWHAL'S "HORN" IS ACTUALLY A TOOTH.

That spiral tusk is a giant, twisty tooth that can grow up to 10 feet long. It sticks straight through the upper lip. Scientists think it helps with sensing, jousting, and looking awesome. Like a sea unicorn!

FACT

THE "SEAL" IN NAVY SEALS STANDS FOR SEA, AIR, AND LAND.

They're trained to operate in all three environments! These elite warriors are so versatile, they can swim underwater, parachute from planes, and trek through tough terrain, all in one mission. Basically, they're like the ultimate "Don't mess with me fighting machines".

JUNE 29

FACT

SOME BIRDS SLEEP WHILE FLYING.

Birds like frigate birds can switch off half their brain at a time and nap mid-flight during long journeys. Not such a big deal though, really, humans can sleep while flying, also, in airplanes.

FACT

THERE'S A TYPE OF RAIN CALLED "BLOOD RAIN".

When dust or red sand gets caught in the clouds, rain can fall looking reddish or rusty. People once thought it was actual blood falling from the sky. Nope, it's just dirty water.

FACT

THE WORD "QUIZ" WAS INVENTED AS A PRANK.

In 1791, a theater manager bet he could make a nonsense word famous overnight. He graffiti-ed "quiz" all over Dublin, and people started using it. Boom. Instant vocabulary.

FACT

WATER CAN BOIL AND FREEZE AT THE SAME TIME.

It's called the triple point, and it happens under just the right temperature and pressure. Science: sometimes it throws a party for all the states of matter.

JULY 3

FACT

THE FIRST PROGRAMMABLE COMPUTER WAS INVENTED IN 1941.

It was invented by Konrad Zuse and was called the Z3. It was designed to perform complex calculations automatically, using punched film as input, making it the world's first fully functional programmable computer. Great! But could it take selfies?

FACT

FIREWORKS WERE INVENTED BY ACCIDENT.

A Chinese cook mixed sulfur, charcoal, and saltpeter and accidentally created gunpowder. Then someone stuffed it into bamboo and BOOM, the first fireworks. Also, it was said that the cook's food tasted terrible. I wonder why?

FACT

THE RAMONES USED TO PLAY 20-MINUTE CONCERTS.

Legendary punk rockers, The Ramones, had songs that were so fast and short, sometimes under two minutes, that they'd blast through their entire set before most bands finished tuning. Punk rock: where speed, sweat, and three chords rule! Oi Oi Oi!

FACT

THERE'S A KIND OF BIRD THAT BUILDS FAKE NESTS TO CONFUSE PREDATORS.

The horned lark creates decoy nests near the real one, just to trick snakes and other sneaky snackers. That's next-level parenting: fake real estate.

JULY 7

FACT

FROGS USE THEIR EYES TO SWALLOW FOOD.

They blink while eating, and their eyes push down into their heads to help shove the food into their throats. So they can actually see if their eyes are bigger than their stomachs.

FACT

THE BOW TIE ORIGINATES FROM CROATIA.

Croatian mercenaries in the 17th century used scarves around their necks to hold their shirts closed. French fashionistas saw it and turned it into a trend. So your classy bow tie started as battlefield gear... and ended up at black-tie galas. From war zone to wardrobe!

JULY 9

FACT

THE WORLD'S OLDEST TOY IS A STICK.

Archaeologists found ancient carved sticks used by kids thousands of years ago. No batteries. No screens. Just a stick. Still popular with dogs today. Mommy, can I have a stick for Christmas?

FACT

FRANCE ONCE BANNED KETCHUP IN SCHOOL CAFETERIAS.

In 2011, the government limited ketchup use in schools, except when served with fries, to make sure students didn't drown traditional French food in tomato sauce. The goal? Keep kids focused on coq au vin, not condiment chaos.

JULY 11

FACT

SOME ANTS FARM APHIDS LIKE HUMANS FARM COWS.

They herd them, protect them, and "milk" them for sweet honeydew. It's like a tiny ant dairy farm. Except everyone is an insect, and no one's wearing overalls.

FACT

YOU CAN'T BURP IN SPACE.

Without gravity, the gas in your stomach doesn't separate from the liquids, so if you try to burp... It's more like a wet surprise. That's why astronauts burp very carefully.

FACT

THE LETTER "J" WASN'T IN THE ALPHABET UNTIL THE 1500S.

The alphabet used to go straight from "I" to "K." The letter J showed up later as a fancy swirl of I. So technically, Julius Caesar was Iulius Caesar. Jnteresting!

FACT

THERE'S A PARASITE THAT REPLACES A FISH'S TONGUE.

The tongue-eating louse latches onto a fish's tongue, eats it, and then becomes the new tongue. It just lives there. Forever. Nature is terrifying and deeply weird.

JULY 15

FACT

SLUGS HAVE GREEN BLOOD.

Some slugs have copper in their blood instead of iron, which makes it green. They're like little gooey aliens. Slime time!

FACT

THE AVERAGE PERSON HAS ENOUGH SALIVA TO FILL TWO SWIMMING POOLS.

Over a lifetime, that's about 25,000 quarts of spit. Gross? Yes. Impressive? Sure! Anyone want to go for a swim in the spit pool?

JULY 17

FACT

THE LARGEST SNOWMAN EVER BUILT WAS OVER 122 FEET TALL.

Built in Maine and nicknamed "Olympia," this snow-woman had trees for arms and tires for buttons. Basically, she was a skyscraper with a carrot.

FACT

ELEPHANTS CAN "HEAR" WITH THEIR FEET.

They detect rumbling sounds through the ground, using their sensitive toe pads. It's like having built-in subwoofers in your toenails. If they can hear with their feet, can they walk with their ears? Maybe not!

JULY 19

FACT

SOMEONE INVENTED A "PET ROCK"... AND BECAME A MILLIONAIRE.

In 1975, Gary Dahl sold smooth stones in little boxes with air holes and straw, as if they were live pets. Each came with a care manual full of jokes like "commands your rock will never follow." It was meant as a joke... but he sold over 1.5 million Pet Rocks. That's right, he got rich selling rocks in a box.

FACT

THE LONGEST-RUNNING GAME SHOW IS THE PRICE IS RIGHT.

It started in 1956 and is still going strong! That means generations of people have learned the price of dish soap and jet skis without ever leaving their Broyhill couch. America's favorite guessing game, with fabulous prizes!

JULY 21

FACT

Someone holds the record for the most snails on their face.

A man in Australia let 43 live snails crawl all over his face for over 10 seconds. No flinching, no sneezing, just maximum slimy composure. He didn't blink, but the snails probably did. If you are gonna be famous for something, this is pretty cool!

FACT

THERE'S A SECRET TRAIN PLATFORM UNDER THE WALDORF ASTORIA HOTEL.

It's called Track 61, and it was built so President Franklin D. Roosevelt could secretly arrive without people seeing that he used a wheelchair. It even had a private elevator from the platform to the hotel. So yes, NYC has a secret presidential Batcave... and it's been hiding under a fancy hotel this whole time.

JULY 23

FACT

DA VINCI COULD WRITE AND DRAW WITH BOTH HANDS AT THE SAME TIME.

He was a left-handed genius who often wrote in mirror script (backwards), just for fun, or maybe to keep his notes secret. Basically, Leonardo Da Vinci was multitasking before it was cool!

FACT

LONDON TAXI DRIVERS HAVE TO MEMORIZE 25000 STREET NAMES.

To become a London black cab driver, you have to pass "The Knowledge", a test where you memorize over 25,000 streets and thousands of landmarks! It takes years of studying and riding a scooter around London to learn every twist and turn. No GPS necessary.

FACT

DURING WORLD WAR II, BRITAIN USED INFLATABLE TANKS.

This was a massive deception plan that included fake armies made of inflatable tanks and wooden airplanes to mislead the Germans about the location of the D-Day invasion. The fake equipment and phantom armies helped convince German forces that the invasion would happen elsewhere. Genius and cheap!

FACT

SOME MONKEYS CAN ROTATE THEIR HEADS ALMOST 180 DEGREES.

Tarsier Monkeys! These tiny, bug-eyed primates can twist their heads like owl ninjas to spot prey. They must be the best at reverse parking!

JULY 27

FACT

DRAGONFLIES CAN FLY IN ALL DIRECTIONS.

Even backward! They're like helicopters with bug eyes. Some species can fly 60 miles per hour, making them the fighter jets of the insect world.

FACT

THE WORLD'S LARGEST PIZZA WAS OVER 13,000 SQUARE FEET.

It took 5 chefs, 13,000 pounds of dough, and a whole lot of sauce. Enough to feed an entire city. Or a hungry teenage girl sleepover party.

FACT

THERE'S A HOUSE MADE WITH A CHAIN-LINK FENCE.

Frank Gehry's own house in Santa Monica started as a simple bungalow, but he transformed it by covering the exterior with unusual materials like chain-link fences, corrugated metal, and plywood scraps! Neighbors complained, which is weird, because their houses used the same materials, just in different places.

FACT

THE SUN IS SO BIG THAT ABOUT 1.3 MILLION EARTHS COULD FIT INSIDE IT!

It's basically a gigantic, glowing ball of hot gas powering our entire solar system. With that much space, the Sun could open the universe's largest nightclub, and still have room for Jupiter to dance.

FACT

THE COUNTRY OF LIECHTENSTEIN ONCE RENTED ITSELF OUT FOR PARTIES.

For a while, you could pay $70,000 a night to "rent" the entire country, flags, fake passports, a parade, and even temporary royalty titles included. Snoop Dogg actually tried to book it for a music video, but they said no. So yes, Liechtenstein was briefly the world's fanciest ballroom.

FACT

WOMBAT POOP IS CUBE-SHAPED.

Seriously. Perfect little poop cubes. Scientists think it helps stop the droppings from rolling away, so wombats can use them to mark their territory. Have you ever thought of a career as a scientist who studies wombat poop?

AUGUST 2

FACT

VENUS IS THE HOTTEST PLANET IN OUR SOLAR SYSTEM.

Even though Mercury is closer to the sun, Venus is still hotter. Venus has a thick, gassy atmosphere that traps heat like a giant greenhouse. The result? Surface temperatures are hot enough to melt lead. If you ever visit, bring sunscreen. And a flameproof suit.

FACT

THERE ARE MORE STARS IN THE UNIVERSE THAN GRAINS OF SAND ON EARTH.

Scientists estimate there are about 1,000 times more stars in the observable universe than all the grains of sand on Earth. So next time you're at the beach, remember: the night sky is way, way bigger and sparklier than your sandy toes!

AUGUST 4

FACT

PARENTS USED TO HANG THEIR BABIES OUT OF APARTMENT WINDOWS.

In New York City, the "Baby Cage" was a real product in the 1930s. It was an outdoor wire cage that parents hung outside apartment windows so babies could get fresh air! It sounds crazy today, but back then, people believed fresh air was the key to health. Those babies must have been covered in pigeon poop.

FACT

THERE'S A KIND OF LIZARD THAT RUNS ON WATER.

The basilisk lizard sprints so fast it stays above the water's surface, earning the nickname "Jesus Lizard." If it wore sneakers, they'd be soaked, but still awesome.

AUGUST 6

FACT

CAMELS HAVE THREE EYELIDS.

To protect their eyes from desert sandstorms, camels have extra eyelids and super-long lashes. Basically, they're walking eyelashes with hooves.

FACT

IN EGYPT, PEOPLE USED TOOTHPASTE MADE OF CRUSHED EGGSHELLS AND ASHES!

They wanted to clean their teeth, but they didn't have the minty toothpaste we use today, so they made their own from whatever they could find. Fresh breath? More like "crunchy charcoal surprise!

AUGUST 8

FACT

TURTLES CAN LIVE OVER 180 YEARS.

The oldest recorded was a Seychelles giant tortoise named Jonathan, who was born in 1832 and is still going strong. There have been 70 wars during his life. He's seen more history than Google.

FACT

YOUR EARS NEVER STOP GROWING.

While most of your body stops growing in your late teens, your ears and nose keep growing for life. Maybe elephants are just really old humans.

AUGUST 10

FACT

SLIME MOLDS CAN SOLVE MAZES.

They're just blobs with no brain, but slime molds can find the fastest path through a maze to get to food. So yes, some yellow goo is smarter than your GPS.

FACT

MOUNT EVEREST IS THE TALLEST MOUNTAIN ABOVE SEA LEVEL.

But it's not the tallest mountain in the world from base to top! A mountain in Hawaii called Mauna Kea is actually taller from its base on the ocean floor to its peak, but most of it is underwater!

AUGUST 12

FACT

THE WORLD'S LARGEST SWIMMING POOL IS OVER 3,000 FEET LONG.

It's longer than 20 Olympic-sized pools put together! It's at a resort in Chile and was built to let people swim and sail in ocean-like water without the waves or sea creatures. It even holds over 66 million gallons of water!

FACT

SEA SPONGES DON'T HAVE BRAINS.

They don't move, think, or have organs. But they filter water and absorb nutrients like peaceful sea squishies. Zero thoughts, just vibes. They are also probably not the best conversationalists either.

FACT

GREENLAND IS MOSTLY COVERED IN ICE, AND ICELAND IS LUSH.

Legend says Viking Erik the Red named Greenland "green" to attract settlers, while Iceland got its chilly name to keep people away. They just swapped names as a clever way to market their lands: Green land is icy, and Ice land is green!

FACT

THE WORLD'S LARGEST LIVING THING IS A FUNGUS.

A honey fungus in Oregon covers over 3.5 miles underground and is over 2,400 years old. It looks like an innocent patch of mushrooms... but it's secretly Earth's largest monster.

AUGUST 16

FACT

SUPERMAN WAS THE FIRST SUPERHERO TO WEAR A CAPE.

It wasn't just for style. His creators gave him a cape partly because the artist thought it would look cool flowing behind him in action, but it also helped make him instantly recognizable and iconic. Superman's cape set the standard for superhero swag everywhere!

FACT

COWS MOO WITH REGIONAL ACCENTS.

Just like humans have different ways of speaking, cows in different areas moo differently. A Texas cow sounds different than a Scottish one. Moo, y'all! I ain't just any ol' cow, I'm pasture prime and fixin' to win Miss Moo-merica!

AUGUST 18

FACT

BASEBALLS USED IN MAJOR LEAGUE GAMES HAVE EXACTLY 108 STITCHES.

The 108 stitches help the ball fly smoothly and give pitchers better control when they throw curves and sliders. Why 108 stitches? Because 107 just was not enough!

FACT

ANTS CAN LIFT 50 TIMES THEIR BODY WEIGHT.

That's like a kid picking up a car. Ants are the ultimate tiny bodybuilders. No gym membership required.

AUGUST 20

FACT

THE ZIPPER WAS FIRST INVENTED WAY BACK IN 1893.

It was kind of a flop at first; it got stuck a lot and didn't work very well. Then, in 1913, a guy named Gideon Sundback made a much better zipper that actually zipped smoothly. Good thing he fixed it; otherwise, our pants would be around our ankles all the time.

FACT

THE OLDEST KNOWN PRINTED BOOK IS THE DIAMOND SUTRA.

It was made in China in the year 868 AD! It was printed using carved wooden blocks to press ink onto paper, which was a super early version of printing before machines were invented.

AUGUST 22

FACT

THERE'S A PLANT THAT SMELLS LIKE ROTTING MEAT.

The corpse flower blooms rarely and smells like a dumpster full of sweaty socks and expired lunch meat. Why? To attract flies for pollination. Nature: sometimes gross, always clever.

FACT

MOST DUST IN YOUR HOME IS MADE OF DEAD SKIN.

About 50–70% of the dust floating around your house is tiny flakes of you. So technically, you're everywhere, even in the lamp and on the toaster.

AUGUST 24

FACT

SPIDERS CAN RE-GROW LOST LEGS.

If a spider loses a leg, it can grow a new one over several molts. It's like self-repair mode... with eight options.

FACT

THE MOON IS SLOWLY DRIFTING AWAY FROM EARTH.

Every year, it moves about 1.5 inches farther away. In a few billion years, say goodbye to tides, dramatic werewolf transformations, and that cool moon car we left up there.

AUGUST 26

FACT

A BLUE WHALE'S TONGUE WEIGHS AS MUCH AS AN ELEPHANT.

A blue whale's tongue is gigantic. Just the tongue alone can weigh up to 8000 pounds (3600 kilograms). They could probably get quite the workout from just eating ice cream cones and lollipops.

FACT

THE "OK" FINGER SIGN MEANS "MONEY" IN JAPAN.

In the USA, making the "ok" sign with your fingers means "good" or "nice". But turn that same sign upside down in Japan, and it means "money". So the next time you are in Japan, and someone asks if you are alright, and you give them the "ok" sign, they may give you some yen.

AUGUST 28

FACT

FLAMINGOS BEND THEIR LEGS THE WRONG WAY.

Or so it seems! What looks like a backward knee is actually their ankle. Their real knees are hidden under feathers. Fashion over function, bird-style.

FACT

THE BIGGEST ART THEFT HAPPENED WITHIN AN HOUR AND A HALF.

In 1990, 13 pieces of art worth over $500 million were stolen from the Isabella Stewart Gardner Museum in Boston, and none have ever been recovered! The mystery remains wide open, and the frames of the art remain empty!

AUGUST 30

FACT

YOU HAVE GOLD IN YOUR BODY.

Your blood contains trace amounts of real gold, about 0.2 milligrams. Not enough to make earrings, but just enough to say you sparkle on the inside.

FACT

THE FASTEST TIME TO EAT A RAW ONION IS 43.53 SECONDS.

It was set by Michelle Lesco in 2017. Eating a whole raw onion, no peeling or slicing tricks, just straight-up onion power in under a minute! No one talked to Michelle for the rest of the day.

SEPTEMBER 1

FACT

A DAY ON EARTH ISN'T EXACTLY 24 HOURS.

It's actually about 23 hours, 56 minutes, and 4 seconds. We round it up for convenience, but technically, every day ends a little early. It's all been a lie!

FACT

SOME METALS CAN BE LIQUID AT ROOM TEMPERATURE.

Gallium melts in your hand, literally. It looks like silver, but turns to goo just above 85°F. Great for science demos, terrible for soup spoons.

SEPTEMBER 3

FACT

THE WORD "ALPHABET" COMES FROM THE FIRST TWO GREEK LETTERS.

They are the letters alpha and beta. Put them together and boom: alphabet. It's like if numbers were called "onetwothreefour."

FACT

YOU CAN'T HUM WHILE HOLDING YOUR NOSE.

Try it. Go ahead. You can't push air out through your nose if it's pinched, and humming is just a nose-powered buzz. Now you look silly, and you're welcome.

SEPTEMBER 5

FACT

THE FIRST VENDING MACHINE WAS INVENTED IN ANCIENT EGYPT.

It dispensed holy water when you dropped in a coin. Charging for holy water seems like a sin.

FACT

BMX STANDS FOR BICYCLE MOTOCROSS.

The "X" isn't just for looking cool (though it totally does), it stands for "cross", as in motocross. So yes, every time you say "BMX," you're secretly speaking extreme biker code. It's like racing slang... in disguise.

SEPTEMBER 7

FACT

THE NUMBER "GOOGOL" IS 1 FOLLOWED BY 100 ZEROS.

It's the number that inspired the name "Google." A googolplex? That's 10 to the power of a googol. Basically, more zeroes than atoms in the universe. Don't even try to count it.

FACT

THE TOWER OF LONDON IS HOME TO RAVENS.

They have been there for hundreds of years, and legend says that if the ravens ever leave, the kingdom will fall. The ravens were kept to protect the Tower and the kingdom, and over time, the story grew that their presence keeps England safe.

SEPTEMBER 9

FACT

THE GREAT WALL OF CHINA IS MORE THAN 13,000 MILES LONG.

That's over five times the distance from New York to Los Angeles. It would take the average human three years to walk it.

FACT

MALE SEAHORSES GIVE BIRTH.

In the weird world of ocean parenting, male seahorses carry the babies. They have a pouch where the female deposits the eggs, and when the babies are ready, he goes into labor. Hundreds of tiny seahorses burst out like confetti. It's a seahorse baby shower.

FACT

IN BHUTAN, TELEVISION WAS COMPLETELY BANNED UNTIL 1999

Bhutan was one of the last countries in the world to allow it. When it was finally introduced, the government worried it might harm traditional culture, so they closely monitored which channels and programs were broadcast.

FACT

PAPER CAN'T BE FOLDED MORE THAN 7-8 TIMES.

No matter the size, the paper gets too thick. But with a giant sheet and a steamroller? A high school student once reached 12 folds. Quite the origami master!

SEPTEMBER 13

FACT

PIGEONS CAN DO MATH.

Pigeons aren't just city-dwelling coo machines, they're clever too! Studies have shown that pigeons can count, sort numbers, and even do simple math problems. Having trouble with math? Hire a pigeon tutor to help and pay them in bread crumbs.

FACT

SATURN'S RINGS ARE DISAPPEARING.

They're slowly raining down onto the planet and may vanish in about 100 million years. So if you want a selfie with them, better book your space trip soon.

SEPTEMBER 15

FACT

YOUR BRAIN RUNS ON ELECTRICITY.

Tiny electrical signals are constantly firing, about 20 watts worth, enough to power a dim light bulb. If you could figure out a way to charge your phone on your head, you'd be a billionaire.

SEPTEMBER 16

FACT

THE WORLD'S DEEPEST POSTBOX IS UNDERWATER IN JAPAN.

It's 10 meters deep, and people actually scuba down to mail letters. I hope those letters are waterproof!

FACT

A SPANISH CHURCH HAS BEEN UNDER CONSTRUCTION FOR 140 YEARS.

Antoni Gaudí, the famous architect from Spain, designed the Sagrada Família church in Barcelona, which has been under construction for over 140 years and is still not finished! Actually, it's not that long. Jonathan the Turtle was born 50 years before construction started, and he's still going.

FACT

THE LONGEST WORD IN ENGLISH HAS 189,819 LETTERS.

It's the name of a protein nicknamed "titin." If you tried to say the full word out loud, it would take 3.5 hours. We'll stick with "titin," thanks.

SEPTEMBER 19

FACT

THE EIFFEL TOWER WAS ALMOST DISMANTLED.

It was supposed to be temporary, but it became so useful for radio signals that they decided to keep it. Paris would have lost 30,000 selfies a day, and some pigeons would be very confused.

FACT

THE OLDEST KNOWN SCHOOL WAS IN EGYPT!

4500 years ago, ancient Egyptians needed to teach kids how to read, write, and do math for jobs like scribes and builders. Imagine trying to pass your history test while history was happening!

SEPTEMBER 21

FACT

ONE SPAGHETTI NOODLE IS CALLED A "SPAGHETTO."

Yep. "Spaghetti" is plural. So when you drop just one noodle on your shirt, you've spilled a spaghetto. Add sauce and you've got yourself a tiny tragedy.

FACT

IT RAINS DIAMONDS ON NEPTUNE AND URANUS.

The extreme pressure turns carbon into diamonds, which fall like glittery hailstones. That's the universe saying, "Here's some fabulous bling weather."

SEPTEMBER 23

FACT

A CIRCLE HAS AN INFINITE NUMBER OF LINES OF SYMMETRY.

A square has exactly four! So, while squares are all about neat, predictable balance, circles are the ultimate shape of perfect symmetry. Is that why New York pizza is better than Detroit pizza?

FACT

THE LONGEST LINE OF SOCKS EVER LAID OUT MEASURED 10,837 SOCKS.

This world record was created in Australia in 2022. They were all clean, matched, and laid end to end, stretching over 8,000 feet (about 1.5 miles), like the world's weirdest, comfiest highway. Why? To raise awareness for Down syndrome and celebrate Lots of Socks Day.

SEPTEMBER 25

FACT

YOU BLINK ABOUT 15-20 TIMES PER MINUTE.

That's over 20,000 blinks a day. Blinking clears away dust, dirt, and microscopic invaders, like a personal janitor working 15-20 times a minute.

FACT

THE LETTER "e" IS THE MOST COMMON LETTER IN ENGLISH.

It appears in about 11% of all words. Poor "z" is over there getting picked last for alphabet dodgeball. If you're ever on that famous game show, remember this fact and buy the vowel "e" first.

SEPTEMBER 27

FACT

SOME ROCKS CAN FLOAT.

Pumice is a type of volcanic rock full of air pockets, so it can float on water. If I had a pumice pet rock, I would call it Bob.

FACT

THERE IS A SHAPE WITH ONLY ONE SIDE.

It's called a Möbius strip. If you twist a strip of paper and tape it into a loop, it has one continuous surface. Try drawing a line without lifting your pencil; it'll loop around forever and drive you crazy, and you'll start trying to lick your elbows.

SEPTEMBER 29

FACT

SOUND TRAVELS FASTER IN WATER THAN IN AIR.

It's about 4 times faster, which is why underwater noises sound extra weird and intense. That's also why dolphins and whales gossip faster than we do.

FACT

THE SPEED OF LIGHT IS THE UNIVERSE'S ULTIMATE SPEED LIMIT.

Nothing (we know of) can go faster than 186,282 miles per second. Even if you were wearing rocket shoes powered by 10,000 gallons of energy drinks, you'd still come in second.

OCTOBER 1

FACT

A PUMPKIN IS TECHNICALLY A FRUIT.

It has seeds and grows from a flower, so it's part of the fruit club, right next to cucumbers, tomatoes, and your idea of a healthy pie.

FACT

THE WORLD'S LARGEST LIBRARY IS THE LIBRARY OF CONGRESS.

It holds over 170 million items, including books, maps, sheet music, and one extremely lost pair of reading glasses.

OCTOBER 3

FACT

IN 1897, A GHOST HELPED SOLVE A MURDER CASE IN THE U.S.!

A woman named Zona Shue was found dead, and her mother claimed her ghost appeared and told her that her husband had killed her. The story convinced authorities to reopen the case... and they found evidence that proved the husband did do it! It's the only U.S. case where ghost testimony helped crack a case.

FACT

ANCIENT ROMANS USED POWDERED MOUSE BRAINS AS TOOTHPASTE.

If you thought using eggshells and ash as toothpaste was gross, the Romans were grosser. Minty fresh? Nope. More like mousy mush. Thankfully, we've upgraded to bubblegum, mint, and baking soda.

OCTOBER 5

FACT

THE FIRST ELECTRIC CAR WAS BUILT AROUND 1888.

It was built by a German inventor named Andreas Flocken. Back then, people wanted cars that were quieter and cleaner than steam or gas engines, so inventors like Flocken worked on electric-powered vehicles. Hmmm...So, where were they for 130 years?

FACT

THE WORD "GHOST" COMES FROM A GERMAN WORD MEANING "SPIRIT".

The German word is "geist," which is easy to remember because it's close to English. The ghost said 'boo.' The Geist said, 'Bitte.' One scared me, the other made me apologize.

OCTOBER 7

FACT

ONE IN EVERY FIVE PEOPLE HAS AN EXTRA RIB.

It's called a cervical rib, and some people don't even know they have it. It's like a surprise bonus level in your skeleton.

FACT

THE EMPIRE STATE BUILDING HAS ITS OWN ZIP CODE.

It's 10118, just for one building. That's when you know your mailbox is kind of a big deal.

OCTOBER 9

FACT

Some types of glass can heal themselves.

Scientists have made self-repairing glass that can fuse back together when pressed. Future phone screens may finally survive your clumsy hands.

FACT

THE CHEESE SLICER WAS INVENTED IN NORWAY.

It was invented in 1925 by Thor Bjørklund, a carpenter from Lillehammer, Norway. He was frustrated that knives cut uneven slices of cheese, so he designed a tool inspired by his woodworking plane. Now everyone can cut the cheese more easily. Thanks, Thor!

OCTOBER 11

FACT

THE ORIGINAL JACK-O'-LANTERNS WERE CARVED FROM TURNIPS.

People in Ireland used turnips and potatoes to ward off evil spirits. Pumpkins showed up later, probably saying, "Hey, I've also got room for a face."

FACT

SPACE SUITS COST AROUND $12 MILLION EACH.

They have about 14 layers to protect astronauts from extreme temperatures, micrometeoroids, and the vacuum of space! So when you see an astronaut, remember, they're basically wearing a tiny, super-expensive spaceship to stay alive!

OCTOBER 13

FACT

THE NUMBER 13 IS FEARED IN MANY PLACES.

In Italy, 17 is the unlucky one. In Korea and Japan, it's 4. So, depending on your passport, the elevator might skip a different floor of doom.

FACT

THE FIRST COMPUTER BUG WAS A REAL INSECT.

In 1947, engineers found a moth inside a computer that was messing things up. They literally "debugged" it. RAM stands for 'Randomly Attracting Moths.

OCTOBER 15

FACT

A museum once hung a painting upside down... for 47 days.

In 1961, New York's Museum of Modern Art accidentally displayed Matisse's "Le Bateau" upside down. No one noticed, not even the art critics. A visitor finally pointed it out, and the museum quietly flipped it back.

FACT

SINGLE PEOPLE IN DENMARK GET CINNAMON THROWN ON THEM.

It's a birthday tradition! If you're still single at 25, your pals might tie you to a pole and blast you with cinnamon powder, sometimes a whole bag. And if you're still single at 30? Pepper time. Cinnamon Danish! YUMMY!

OCTOBER 17

FACT

THE CALENDAR WE USE IS WRONG.

Every year, we drift 26 seconds off true solar time. After a few thousand years, your great-great-grandkids will be celebrating New Year's in the middle of July.

FACT

THERE'S A TYPE OF CLOUD SHAPED LIKE A UFO.

They're called lenticular clouds, and they form over mountains. If you see one and yell, "ALIENS!", you're only half wrong.

OCTOBER 19

FACT

"HELLO" WASN'T THE ORIGINAL PHONE GREETING.

Alexander Graham Bell wanted us to say "Ahoy!" when answering the phone. Can you imagine your teacher calling, and you going full pirate?

FACT

YOUR TEETH ARE JUST AS UNIQUE AS YOUR FINGERPRINTS.

No two people have the exact same set of teeth! That's why dentists can use teeth for identification, and why your smile is one-of-a-kind. Imagine if your teeth were used for airport security: 'Please bite this scanner'.

OCTOBER 21

FACT

A PERSON WALKS AS MUCH IN A LIFETIME AS FIVE TRIPS AROUND EARTH.

That's about 110,000 miles. Walked around the Earth 5 times and still can't find where I left my keys.

FACT

SLOTHS CAN HOLD THEIR BREATH LONGER THAN DOLPHINS!

You'd think dolphins, who live in water, would win this contest. But sloths are secretly breath-holding champs. They can slow down their heart rate and hold their breath for up to 40 minutes! Dolphins usually need air every 10 to 15 minutes. It might be profitable to train sloths to dive for pearls.

OCTOBER 23

FACT

THE WORLD'S LARGEST BUBBLEGUM BUBBLE WAS 20 INCHES (50.8 CM).

It was blown by Chad Fell in 2004, and get this, he didn't use his hands to shape it! Just pure lung power. Blowing a bubble that big without popping it is like trying to hold a tiny balloon made of chewing gum, totally wild and sticky!

OCTOBER 24

FACT

YOUR PHONE IS SMARTER THAN THE COMPUTERS USED FOR APOLLO 11.

The Apollo 11 guidance system was a weakling compared to your TikTok machine. Use that power wisely.

OCTOBER 25

FACT

THERE'S A WORD FOR WHEN YOU CAN'T REMEMBER A WORD.

I can not remember that word, though. Just kidding! Lethologica is the word. It's that feeling of "it 's-on-the-tip-of-my-tongue".

Ironically, "lethologica" is a word you'll probably forget.

FACT

SOME MIRRORS FLIP YOUR REFLECTION UPSIDE DOWN.

A concave mirror, like the ones in amusement parks, reflects you upside down when you're far away. Reality distortion, brought to you by science.

OCTOBER 27

FACT

BOREDOM IS GOOD FOR CREATIVITY.

Studies show that daydreaming activates parts of your brain linked to problem-solving and imagination. So, zoning out in math class? You're secretly inventing time travel.

FACT

A CROCODILE CAN GO MONTHS WITHOUT EATING.

Crocodiles have slow metabolisms and can live off one big meal for months. In extreme cases, they've gone over a year without food. That's like eating one pizza and being full until next summer. Cheap date!

OCTOBER 29

FACT

A GROUP OF WITCHES IS CALLED A "COVEN."

In the 1600s, during the height of witch-hunting hysteria in Europe and later in Scotland and England, the word "coven" started being used specifically to describe a gathering of witches. Thirteen spellcasters = instant coven.

FACT

HUMANS SHED 30,000 TO 40,000 SKIN CELLS PER MINUTE.

That's about 9 pounds of skin per year. The outer layer of your skin is made of cells that are constantly exposed to the sun, germs, sweat, air, and your questionable snack choices. So the body replaces them regularly, like a boss. You're a snow globe of yourself.

OCTOBER 31

FACT

HALLOWEEN IS OVER 2,000 YEARS OLD.

It started as a Celtic festival called Samhain, marking the end of harvest and the belief that ghosts could cross into our world.

Trick-or-treating came much later. Ghosts were the OG candy collectors.

FACT

IN THE 1950S, SOMEONE INVENTED THE "MOTORIZED ICE CREAM CONE".

It was a cone with a tiny motor inside that would rotate the ice cream so you didn't have to lick it yourself! It was meant to be a hands-free way to enjoy ice cream, but it never became popular. If you can't lick your cone manually, that's just lazy.

NOVEMBER 2

FACT

THE HASHTAG SYMBOL IS ACTUALLY CALLED AN "OCTOTHORPE."

No one's quite sure why. "Octo" means eight (for the points), and "thorpe" was possibly added just because it sounded cool. So yes, every time you use #TacoTuesday, you're using ancient nonsense slang.

FACT

THE FIRST SIGHTING OF THE LOCH NESS MONSTER WAS IN 565 AD.

It was when an Irish monk wrote about a "water beast" in the area! That means Nessie has been part of local legends for over 1,500 years, long before cameras or tourists showed up. A monster with serious staying power!

NOVEMBER 4

FACT

THERE'S A BASKETBALL COURT IN THE U.S. SUPREME COURT BUILDING.

It's nicknamed the "Highest Court in the Land." It's literally above the actual courtroom. Justice... with a jump shot.

FACT

THE WORD "BOOKKEEPER" HAS THREE PAIRS OF DOUBLE LETTERS IN A ROW.

oo, kk, ee. No other word in English does that. It's like a secret club for vowels and consonants who walk in two-by-two.

NOVEMBER 6

FACT

THE "ZIP" IN ZIP CODE STANDS FOR ZONE IMPROVEMENT PLAN.

Which sounds fancy, but basically just means "faster mail." Sorry, no actual zipping involved. Add that to the pot of useless information and pull it out when there's an awkward silence.

FACT

YOUR PINKY FINGER PROVIDES 50% OF YOUR HAND'S STRENGTH.

Tiny but mighty! Pinky strength is real. It holds your coffee mug, your secrets, and your entire childhood honor code.

NOVEMBER 8

FACT

SOME FROGS CAN HOLD THEIR PEE FOR EIGHT MONTHS.

The wood frog in Alaska can go pee-free for most of the year. It stores up waste in its body to help survive the freezing winter, then finally lets it all out when spring arrives. Oh, what a relief that spring pee must be!

FACT

EINSTEIN DIDN'T SPEAK UNTIL HE WAS 4 YEARS OLD.

Some worried he might have learning difficulties, but he later became one of history's greatest geniuses! Sometimes, slow starters end up changing the world.

NOVEMBER 10

FACT

LIGHT TAKES 8 MINS. AND 20 SEC. TO REACH EARTH FROM THE SUN.

So when you wave at the sun, the photons hitting your face left before your last math class ended. The Sun's like, 'I sent you light 8 minutes ago. Are you just now opening it? Rude.

FACT

THE LETTER "Q" IS ALMOST ALWAYS FOLLOWED BY A "U" IN ENGLISH.

Except in a few weird words like qat and qindarka. Which are real words, even if your spelling bee judge gasps.

NOVEMBER 12

FACT

INDIA MAKES THE MOST MOVIES IN THE WORLD.

India makes over 1,000 a year, almost three a day. They're made in many languages and often include songs and dances that can happen anytime, even during serious moments. Action!

Actor 1: My turtle ran away.

Actor 2: I'm so sorry! Let's dance!

FACT

A GOOGLE SEARCH USES MORE POWER THAN THE APOLLO 11 MISSION.

Apollo 11 landed on the Moon with 64 KB of memory. You: Need 64 GB just to check your email without freezing. That means Googling "how to toast bread" is more powerful than the computer that landed humans on the Moon. Priorities!

NOVEMBER 14

FACT

THE POPSICLE WAS INVENTED BY ACCIDENT BY AN 11-YEAR-OLD.

Frank Epperson, in 1905, left a cup of soda mixed with a stick outside overnight, and it froze! He called it the "Epsicle" at first, but it was later renamed "popsicle" and became a summertime favorite for kids everywhere. A delicious happy accident!

FACT

ZAHA HADID WAS THE FIRST WOMAN TO WIN THE PRITZKER PRIZE.

The Pritzker Architecture Prize is often called the "Nobel Prize of architecture,". Architect Zaha Hadid was famous for her futuristic, curvy designs that looked like they were from another planet.

NOVEMBER 16

FACT

Someone invented a helmet for chickens.

In 2014, the company Kritter Kommunity created tiny chicken helmets to protect hens from pecking and getting attacked by predators; some helmets were glittery, while others were spiked. Now, rare collectors' items it just proves that if it exists, someone will accessorize it.

FACT

YOU HAVE ABOUT 2 TO 5 MILLION SWEAT GLANDS ALL OVER YOUR BODY!

When you sweat, your body can produce up to 1 gallon (around 4 liters) of sweat per hour during intense exercise or heat to help cool you down. Nature's own air conditioning!

NOVEMBER 18

FACT

UNCOPYRIGHTABLE IS THE LONGEST WORD WITH NO REPEATED LETTERS.

Every letter appears once. Maybe it's not the most used word in the English language (unless you are a publisher), but when it is used, it's the equivalent of a mic drop.

FACT

HUMANS SHARE ABOUT 60% OF THEIR DNA WITH FRUIT FLIES.

Scientists study fruit flies to learn about human health because those little guys can get versions of the same diseases we do. If one lands on your apple, remember: you're kind of related. Ew.

NOVEMBER 20

FACT

A SHARK CAN REPLACE OVER 30,000 TEETH IN ITS LIFETIME.

They have rows of backup teeth that keep growing and moving forward. They must have expensive dentist bills.

FACT

THE OLDEST KNOWN FISHING HOOKS ARE OVER 23,000 YEARS OLD!

They were made from bone and found in East Timor, showing that humans have been fishing for a really, really long time. We have been fishing for that long, but we still get our lines all tangled up.

FACT

ANCIENT GREEKS THOUGHT SNEEZES WERE SIGNS FROM THE GODS.

This is because sneezing was seen as a sudden, uncontrollable event that seemed to come from beyond human control, kind of like a divine interruption. Which means someone probably once yelled, "Bless you, Zeus!" across a marketplace.

FACT

THERE ARE MORE POSSIBLE MOVES IN A GAME OF CHESS THAN ATOMS.

In the observable universe, anyway. That's about 10^120 possible positions. I tried to plan my chess moves and accidentally booked a flight to confusion island.

NOVEMBER 24

FACT

YOU CAN'T LICK YOUR OWN ELBOW.

Only about 1% of people can actually lick their elbow, usually because they have unusually long tongues or super bendy arms. Most people can't, anyway. Now you're trying it, aren't you? It's OK. We all tried. Welcome to the elbow club.

FACT

IN AUSTRALIA, IT ONCE RAINED SPIDERS.

In 2015, residents of a town in New South Wales reported thousands of tiny spiders falling from the sky and covering everything with silky webs. It's a real phenomenon called ballooning, where spiders use their silk to catch the wind and travel long distances, sometimes all at once!

NOVEMBER 26

FACT

THE SHORTEST COMPLETE SENTENCE IN ENGLISH IS "GO."

It's a full sentence with a subject (you) and a verb (go). If Shakespeare wrote 'Go,' it'd be the most dramatic two-letter play ever.

FACT

THE ORIGINAL MONOPOLY GAME WAS CIRCULAR.

Invented in 1903, The Landlord's Game used a round board to show the endless cycle of rent. Monopoly: because sometimes, destroying friendships over fake money is the best family bonding.

NOVEMBER 28

FACT

NOVEMBER USED TO BE THE NINTH MONTH.

In Latin, "novem" means nine. Then January and February were added later. November is the reason your jeans suddenly feel like they shrank in the dryer. Thank you, Thanksgiving!

FACT

THE PANAMA CANAL USES GRAVITY, NOT PUMPS, TO MOVE SHIPS.

The entire lock system relies on a brilliant feat of engineering: millions of gallons of water are moved using gravity alone. Water from man-made lakes flows in and out of the locks to raise or lower ships like a giant aquatic elevator. No motors required to fill the chambers!

NOVEMBER 30

FACT

THE FIRST ELECTRIC GUITAR WAS INVENTED IN THE EARLY 1930S.

Invented by George Beauchamp, who co-founded the company that became Fender! Before that, guitars were mostly acoustic and quiet, but the electric guitar changed music forever. Rock ‘n’ roll was born! And parents got scared.

FACT

SNOW ISN'T WHITE.

Snowflakes are actually clear, but they scatter light in all directions, making them look white. It's like a frozen disco ball party, but quieter.

DECEMBER 2

FACT

KANGAROOS CAN'T WALK BACKWARD.

Their big feet and muscular tails are awesome for hopping forward, but totally useless for backing up. So never try to back a kangaroo in a corner, it won't work.

FACT

"JINGLE BELLS" WAS THE FIRST SONG PLAYED IN SPACE.

In 1965, astronauts pranked Mission Control by reporting a UFO... then played "Jingle Bells" on a harmonica and sleigh bells. Space: now available with holiday cheer.

DECEMBER 4

FACT

THE LONGEST WORD YOU CAN TYPE WITH JUST YOUR LEFT HAND IS "STEWARDESSES."

On a QWERTY keyboard, all the letters in the word stewardesses are on the left, so your left hand is doing all the heavy lifting, and it still sounds like airplane royalty.

FACT

IN MEDIEVAL EUROPE, PEOPLE ATE MUMMIES.

The mummies were ground into a powder and eaten. This strange practice, called mumia, was thought to cure all kinds of ailments and was sold as medicine for centuries. What's for dinner? Grandma or Grandpa?

DECEMBER 6

FACT

BABY PUFFINS ARE CALLED PUFFLINGS.

Let's just take a second to admire that word: puffling. It's real, it's adorable, and it sounds like something from a magical storybook. Pufflings live in burrows, flap their tiny wings, and eventually grow into stylish adult puffins.

DECEMBER 7

FACT

PENCILS DON'T ACTUALLY CONTAIN LEAD.

They're filled with graphite, a form of carbon. Graphite: the safe, artsy cousin of lead who lets you shade, sketch, and still fail math.

DECEMBER 8

FACT

SKIING IS ONE OF THE OLDEST MODES OF TRANSPORTATION.

Archaeologists have found ski-like wooden planks dating back over 8,000 years in what is now Russia and Scandinavia! People originally used skis to travel across snowy landscapes long before it became a popular sport or recreation.

FACT

THERE'S A MUSEUM IN SWEDEN DEVOTED ENTIRELY TO FAILURES.

The Museum of Failure features flops like ketchup-flavored cereal and candy corn cookies. It's proof that bad ideas can still win awards.

DECEMBER 10

FACT

Some snowflakes are shaped like needles, not stars.

Snow comes in at least 35 official shapes, including columns, plates, and weird frozen spaghetti. They're snowflakes with attitude, 'I'm cold and I'm sharp, deal with it.

FACT

THE SMELL OF BOOKS IS CALLED "BIBLIOSMIA."

It's the mix of chemicals from paper, ink, and age. That old book smell? That would be an interesting scent for deodorant.

DECEMBER 12

FACT

THE STATUE OF LIBERTY'S FULL NAME IS LIBERTY ENLIGHTENING THE WORLD.

The name wasn't just poetic; it reflected a vision of freedom, enlightenment, and international unity. So the next time someone says "Statue of Liberty," bring up this nugget and watch their expression change.

FACT

PIGS CAN LEARN TO PLAY VIDEO GAMES.

In one experiment, pigs were trained to use a joystick with their snouts to play simple games, like guiding a cursor to a target. They were surprisingly good at it, too! Scientists say pigs are smarter than dogs in many ways. But at least dogs know how not to get eaten.

DECEMBER 14

FACT

THE EARTH IS CLOSEST TO THE SUN IN EARLY JANUARY.

Wait, what? Yep. Even though it's cold in the Northern Hemisphere, Earth actually reaches its perihelion in January. Blame the seasons on tilt, not distance.

FACT

THE ROLLING STONES GOT THEIR NAME FROM A SONG.

It was by blues legend Muddy Waters. Their original band name was The Rollin' Stones (without the "g")! They changed it later to sound cooler, but it's funny to think the name started as a simple tribute and evolved into one of rock's most famous brands.

DECEMBER 16

FACT

THE WORD "NERD" FIRST APPEARED IN A DR. SEUSS BOOK.

In *If I Ran the Zoo* (1950), he wrote: "And then, just to show them, I'll sail to Ka-Troo / And bring back an It-Kutch, a Preep and a Proo, / A Nerkle, a Nerd, and a Seersucker too." The rest is glasses-wearing, pocket protector history.

FACT

ANTARCTICA IS THE DRIEST DESERT ON EARTH.

A desert doesn't have to be only sand; it's just a place that receives little rain. Antarctica may be covered in ice, but it gets less than 2 inches of precipitation a year. It's basically a giant frozen raisin.

DECEMBER 18

FACT

AN ANT CAN SURVIVE IN A MICROWAVE.

You'd think the microwave zaps everything, but ants can dodge the microwaves by walking around and avoiding the hot spots. Their small size helps, too. WARNING! Do not try this experiment at home. You may get ants in your pants or become the King of France.

DECEMBER 19

FACT

YOU'RE TALLER IN THE MORNING.

Thanks to gravity squishing your spine all day, you shrink about half an inch by bedtime. So enjoy your peak height while brushing your teeth.

DECEMBER 20

FACT

TINSEL WAS ORIGINALLY MADE OF REAL SILVER.

Back in the 1600s, in Germany, people draped actual shredded silver on their trees. Festive, yes. Friendly on the wallet? Not at all. Must've been nice to be rich back then!

FACT

THE SHORTEST DAY OF THE YEAR IS DECEMBER 21.

It's the Winter Solstice, and it has the fewest hours of sunlight. Good day for cocoa, couch forts, and wondering if the sun hit snooze.

DECEMBER 22

FACT

"XMAS" ISN'T TAKING THE "CHRIST" OUT OF CHRISTMAS.

The letter "X" is from the Greek letter Chi, which is the first letter of "Christos" (Christ). So "Xmas" is just... Greek shorthand. Ancient texting.

FACT

THERE'S A JELLYFISH THAT CAN LIVE FOREVER.

Meet Turritopsis dohrnii, also known as the "immortal jellyfish." When it's injured or old, it can turn its body back into a baby jellyfish, starting its life all over again. It's like pressing the restart button on life, over and over. Scientists are still trying to figure out how it pulls off this watery magic trick.

DECEMBER 24

FACT

THE NORAD SANTA TRACKER STARTED WITH THE WRONG PHONE NUMBER.

In 1955, a newspaper accidentally printed the phone number for NORAD (a military base) as Santa's. They went with it, and now millions of kids track Santa every Christmas Eve. Ho-ho-whoops!

FACT

CHRISTMAS WASN'T ALWAYS ON DECEMBER 25.

Early Christians didn't celebrate it at all, and the exact date of Jesus's birth isn't known. December 25 was chosen later, possibly to match winter festivals. So technically, Santa rescheduled history.

DECEMBER 26

FACT

EARTH'S ROTATION IS SLOWING DOWN.

By about 1.7 milliseconds per century. So in 140 million years, days will be 25 hours long. One more hour to scroll aimlessly! Yay!

FACT

THE COLDEST TEMPERATURE EVER RECORDED WAS -128.6°F.

It happened in Antarctica in 1983. That's so cold, your eyebrows would freeze into quotation marks ' '. Even Frosty the Snowman was like, 'Nope, I'm out.'.

DECEMBER 28

FACT

THE LARGEST SNOWFLAKE EVER RECORDED WAS 15 INCHES WIDE.

It fell in Montana in 1887 and was reportedly the size of a frozen pizza. You don't catch that snowflake on your tongue, you catch it with an umbrella and a helmet.

FACT

THE HUMAN BODY GIVES OFF ENOUGH HEAT TO BOIL WATER.

If you captured all the body heat from a human, you could boil a liter of water in about 1.5 hours. My workout could double as pasta prep.

FACT

TIME ZONES ARE NOT STRAIGHT LINES.

They wiggle around countries, cities, and even islands that want to party early. Some places are 15 minutes ahead of their neighbors. One step to the left: it's 3 p.m. One step to the right: it's next Thursday.

FACT

NEW YEAR'S EVE IS CELEBRATED AT 38 DIFFERENT TIMES AROUND THE WORLD.

Because of time zones, the new year rolls out like a global wave. It takes 26 hours for the whole planet to finish yelling "Happy New Year!" So technically, the party never ends. Now your brain is full of fun facts. Happy New Year!

Short & Silly
JOKES
What do you call a fish that wears a bow tie?
SO-FISH-TICATED
ONE CHEESY JOKE A DAY FOR A YEAR
For Kids 8-12

ABOUT THE AUTHOR

ALBERT B. SQUID

If you spot this person please call our HOTLINE at 867-5309 ask for Tommy.

Born to a family of construction peeps, ALBERT B. SQUID was raised on construction sites in Massachusetts. Believe it or not, he holds two degrees in Engineering and Architecture and has worked as an Architect in Boston, Tokyo, and Seoul. In the year 2000, Squid started an independent children's book publishing company in NYC. I had fun doing that.....I mean HE (Albert B. Squid) had fun doing that! After becoming a freelance voice actor, the elusive author's whereabouts are unknown. He was last seen in the town of Shaike in the East African country of Djibouti learning traditional disco dance. Squid recommends if you go to Shaike, Djibouti get lessons from the dance teacher named K.C.

albertbsquid.com

www.ingramcontent.com/pod-product-compliance
Lightning Source LLC
Chambersburg PA
CBHW062114020426
42335CB00013B/955

* 9 7 8 1 9 5 9 2 0 9 5 0 8 *